# DON'T L(

# DON'T LOOK BACK

## 8 sessions on living out your commitment to Christ

## David P. Seemuth

**VICTOR BOOKS**

A DIVISION OF SCRIPTURE PRESS PUBLICATIONS INC.
USA CANADA ENGLAND

Most Scripture quotations are from the *Holy Bible, New International Version®*. Copyright © 1973, 1978, 1984 by International Bible Society. Used by permission of Zondervan Publishing House. All rights reserved.

Editor: Pamela T. Campbell
Designer: Joe DeLeon
Cover Illustration: Richard McNeel
Interior Illustration: Al Hering

Recommended Dewey Decimal Classification: 301.402
Suggested Subject Heading: SMALL GROUPS

Library of Congress Catalog Card Number: 92-061273
ISBN: 1-56476-032-4

1   2   3   4   5   6   7   8   9   10 Printing / Year   96   95   94   93   92

VICTOR BOOKS
A division of SP Publications, Inc.
        Wheaton, Illinois 60187

# CONTENTS

**PURPOSE:** To become committed disciples.

# INTRODUCTION

*Don't Look Back* is for people who want to know more about how to live out their commitment to Christ. An in-depth Leader's Guide is included at the back of the book with suggested time guidelines to help you structure your emphases. Each of the 8 sessions contains the following elements:

❑ **GroupSpeak**—quotes from group members that capsulize what the session is about.

❑ **Getting Acquainted**—activities or selected readings to help you begin thinking and sharing from your life and experiences about the subject of the session. Use only those options that seem appropriate for your group.

❑ **Gaining Insight**—questions and in-depth Bible study help you gain principles from Scripture for life-related application.

❑ **Growing By Doing**—an opportunity to practice the Truth learned in the Gaining Insight section.

❑ **Going The Second Mile**—a personal enrichment section for you to do on your own.

❑ **Growing As A Leader**—an additional section in the Leader's Guide for the development and assessment of leadership skills.

❑ **Pocket Principles**—brief guidelines inserted in the Leader's Guide to help the Group Leader learn small group leadership skills as needed.

❑ **Session Objectives**—goals listed in the Leader's Guide that describe what should happen in the group by the end of the session.

# IS THIS YOUR FIRST SMALL GROUP?

**'smol grüp:**    A limited number of individuals assembled together having some unifying relationship.

**Kris'chən**    4–12 persons who meet together on a regular ba-
**'smol grüp:**    sis, over a determined period of time, for the shared purpose of pursuing biblical truth. They seek to mature in Christ and become equipped to serve as His ministers in the world.

*Picture Your First Small Group.*

List some words that describe what you want your small group to look like.

## What Kind Of Small Group Do You Have?
People form all kinds of groups based on gender, age, marital status, and so forth. There are advantages and disadvantages to each. Here are just a few:

❏ **Same Age Groups** will probably share similar needs and interests.

- ❏ **Intergenerational Groups** bring together people with differ-ent perspectives and life experiences.

- ❏ **Men's or Women's Groups** usually allow greater freedom in sharing and deal with more focused topics.

- ❏ **Singles or Married Groups** determine their relationship em-phases based on the needs of a particular marital status.

- ❏ **Mixed Gender Groups (singles and/or couples)** stimulate interaction and broaden viewpoints while reflecting varied lifestyles.

However, the most important area of "alikeness" to consider when forming a group is an **agreed-on purpose**. Differences in purpose will sabotage your group and keep its members from bonding. If, for example, Mark wants to pray but not play while Jan's goal is to learn through playing, then Mark and Jan's group will probably not go anywhere. People need different groups at different times in their lives. Some groups will focus on sharing and accountability, some on work projects or service, and others on worship. *Your small group must be made up of persons who have similar goals.*

## How Big Should Your Small Group Be?
The **fewest** people to include would be **4**. Accountability will be high, but absenteeism may become a problem.

The **most** to include would be **12**. But you will need to subdivide regularly into groups of 3 or 4 if you want people to feel cared for and to have time for sharing.

## How Long Should You Meet?
**8 Weeks** gives you a start toward becoming a close community but doesn't overburden busy schedules. Count on needing three or four weeks to develop a significant trust level. The smaller the group, the more quickly trust develops.

**Weekly Meetings** will establish bonding at a good pace and allow for accountability. The least you can meet and still be an effective group is once a month. If you choose the latter, work at individual contact among group members between meetings.

You will need **75 minutes** to accomplish a quality meeting. The larger the size, the more time it takes to become a healthy group. Serving refreshments will add 20–30 minutes, and singing and/or prayer time, another 20–30 minutes. Your time duration may be determined by the time of day you meet and by the amount of energy members bring to the group. Better to start small and ask for more time when it is needed because of growth.

## What Will Your Group Do?

To be effective, each small group meeting should include:

1. **Sharing**—You need to share who you are and what is happening in your life. This serves as a basis for relationship building and becomes a springboard for searching out scriptural truth.

2. **Scripture**—There must always be biblical input from the Lord to teach, rebuke, correct, and train in right living. Such material serves to move your group in the direction of maturity in Christ and protects from pooled ignorance and distorted introspection.

3. **Truth in practice**—It is vital to provide opportunities for *doing* the Word of God. Experiencing this within the group insures greater likelihood that insights gained will be utilized in everyday living.

Other elements your group may wish to add to these three are: a time of **worship, specific prayer** for group members, **shared projects**, a time to **socialize** and enjoy **refreshments**, and **recreation.**

# ONE

## *Priorities*

**GroupSpeak:** *"Sometimes I'm tempted to think of God's will as something that's always opposed to my will. But lately I've been pleasantly surprised to find that my deepest desires—for love, joy, peace—are exactly the things God wants to give me. Maybe I've learned to stop fighting it so much."*

### Something Always Comes Up!

A radio announcer once asked Leo Durocher, who managed the Chicago Cubs at the time, "Barring the unforseen, Leo, will you win the Pennant?"

Durocher replied: "There ain't gonna be no unforseen."

But how many times have your plans gone just exactly as you envisioned them unfolding? How many times did the unforseen serve to get you into a significant time bind? Then what?

We rarely meet anyone who is satisfied with the amount of time he or she has to accomplish all that needs to be done. We are constantly saying, "If only I had time to . . ." When questioned we usually come back to the need to prioritize our time better. And that will probably be a constant struggle; our

**13**

society pulls us in different directions. It is so easy to lose sight of what is really important.

Setting wise, Christian priorities is the theme of this first session. It will be a challenging session, surely, since we all struggle to a greater or lesser degree in this area. Though His words, upon first hearing, may sound harsh, Jesus gives us direction that will make our walks as disciples a little bit easier. Are we really ready to follow Christ diligently?

## GETTING ACQUAINTED

**Reaching the Top**

Share your name with the group and describe someone you admire who has reached the top of a field/profession/endeavor. What accomplishments tell you that the person has indeed "reached the top"?

What are some of the things this person had to do to reach the pinnacle?

What sacrifices did this person likely have to make?

Why do you admire this person? What personal qualities does she or he have that you would like to acquire?

What is your personal vision of what it means for you to "reach the top," or be "successful"?

Name two or three things that tend to hinder you as you pursue this goal.

## GAINING INSIGHT

**Following Jesus**
Read Luke 9:57-62.

⁵⁷**As they were walking along the road, a man said to Him, "I will follow you wherever you go." ⁵⁸Jesus replied, "Foxes have holes and birds of the air have nests, but the Son of Man has no place to lay his head." ⁵⁹He said to another man, "Follow me." But the man replied, "Lord, first let me go bury my father." ⁶⁰Jesus said to him, "Let the dead bury their own dead, but you go and proclaim the kingdom of God." ⁶¹Still another said, "I will follow you Lord; but first let me go back and say good-by to my family." ⁶²Jesus replied, "No one who puts his hand to the plow and looks back is fit for service in the kingdom of God."**

**Luke 9:57-62**

Jesus did not hold back when people inquired about following Him. He wanted them to know exactly what kind of commitment He required. One might say that Jesus knew how to live and attracted a band of followers who wished to emulate Him. He was able to show, through real-life examples what a difference wise, kingdom-centered priorities can make. We need to learn those same priorities.

Luke shows what it means to be a committed follower of Jesus through sharing three of Jesus' encounters with would-be followers. How would you describe your basic reaction to Jesus' statements in Luke 9:57-62?

_____ Considerably confusing: What does He mean?
_____ Definitely demanding: No way I could live up to this.
_____ Disconcertingly discouraging: Makes me want to give up.
_____ Exquisitely exciting: Alright! I love a challenge!

**15**

_____ Blissfully boring: Ho-Hum ... I've heard it all before.
_____ Ingeniously insightful: Rings true with my feelings about discipleship.
_____ Other:_____

Summarize in your own words the point Jesus is making in these verses:

Luke 9:58




Luke 9:60




Luke 9:62




There is no question about it. Jesus' words are tough to swallow. They seem to be so extreme. Can Jesus really be serious about such drastic commitment? Is this the kind of commitment evident in your church? In your life? If not, what is the best way for Christians to begin making changes toward greater commitment and more Christ-like priorities? Discuss some practical ideas with the other group members. Strive to keep your suggestions "down to earth" and focused on "real life," as the biblical examples were.

Description of a "committed Christian life"

❏ At work


❏ At home

❑ In my neighborhood

❑ With my relatives

❑ At play

❑ At church

In 1 Corinthians 1:18 the Apostle Paul declares that the Gospel is "foolishness to those who are perishing, but to us who are being saved it is the power of God." In what way is the Gospel "foolishness" to your unbelieving friends, relatives, coworkers, and neighbors?

What is a Christian, according to Acts 11:25-26? Do we have the same understanding of what a Christian is in our day?

What is the essence of discipleship according to Matthew 10:39?

What does it mean, to you personally, to "lose" your life? To "find" your life? On a scale of 1 to 10, to what degree are you doing both? Mark the scale, and explain your response to the other group members.

| 1 | 2 | 3 | 4 | 5 | 6 | 7 | 8 | 9 | 10 |
|---|---|---|---|---|---|---|---|---|---|

I am "losing" my old life                              I am "finding" my new life
and its self-centered priorities          and its Christ-centered priorities

**17**

God expects a lot from us, His children. Yet many of us fear greater commitment to Jesus because we are afraid of what we may have to give up. That is exactly what setting priorities involves: We must give up one thing in order to do another. For example, your involvement with your small group is a way of following through with your priority of growing in Christ. You had to put aside something else in order to be a part of this group. (No one has "extra time" to attend a small group!) We make such time a priority. It is a practical way of living out your commitment to Jesus Christ.

## GROWING BY DOING

### Considering Total Commitment
From the biblical descriptions of discipleship, following the Lord sounds tough. Is it? Why or why not?

In your group discuss specific issues such as: maintaining Christian priorities in your business, in your home, in your heart, in your leisure, etc. For each area, try to answer this question: "What would a committed Christian life 'look like' in this area?" Be as realistic as possible about what things in your life might need to change and what things would likely stay the same.

How would the church be different if people took these teachings more seriously? Share some examples that come to mind.

What would the attitude of our family be if we began living more in line with Christ's priorities?

What holds us back from the type of commitment Jesus spoke of?

In groups of three or four answer the following: What do you need to do to keep the proper set of "kingdom priorities" in view during your daily routines? Talk in your group about what things you could do personally in your home, church, work, neighborhood, leisure time, or in other relationships to put your ideas into practice. Choose one area and be specific about how you could work on changing your attitudes and/or actions to bring them in line with biblical priorities. Share with the group, asking for prayer to help you follow through.

## GOING THE SECOND MILE

**Thinking About Your Group**
Who in your group exhibits some admirable ways of handling priorities? How can you learn from his/her example? List two or three questions here that you would like to ask this person (perhaps by phone, during the week) about his/her approach to Christian discipleship:

**Thinking About Yourself**
Is there an area of your life that you would like to change in order to become a more devoted follower of Jesus? How can you make those changes in your life? Who can you look to for encouragement and prayer as you pursue those changes?

Don't overwhelm yourself with unrealistic goals! Decide on one small step you could take this week to move yourself closer to Christ in the area of time use and priorities. Make a brief note about your plan.




### Thinking About Your World
Imagine being a person that you know—perhaps a non-believer friend—that you "rub elbows" with regularly. How would you say this person views your priorities in life? Complete the following statement as your non-Christian friend would:

"I see _____ (your name) as being mostly interested in _____

_____ .
In fact, this seems to be the center of _____ 's life."

Think: To what extent does my friend's view of me show that I am living by Christian values and priorities? What is the overall impact of my lifestyle on my friend?

# TWO

## *Focus*

**GroupSpeak:** *"It helps me to think of God's discipline in terms of 'correction' rather than 'punishment.' That way I realize that God is helping me learn and grow instead of being down on me when I fail. I know He's proud of me, just like I'm proud of my own children. He's just helping me re-focus on what's important."*

### Clear or Blurry?

"Oh no! Not again! I can't even tell if that's Uncle Bud or Aunt Alice! And is that your hat, or did a squirrel jump on your head?" We have all experienced those times when we get a roll of film back from the developing processors and find the majority of the pictures out of focus. If we are truly "amateurs" when it comes to photography, and we find five or six really good pictures, most of us are delighted. Auto-focus cameras are truly remarkable since they correct our mistakes in this most crucial area of photography: focus.

It is too bad our lives don't have an "auto-focus" mode. Wouldn't it be wonderful if we were able to push a button and instantly our hearts and minds would focus on the Lord Jesus Christ. A life out of focus is like the blurry picture—it's hard to see one's inner beauty coming through, or God's hand at work. But a life lived in the clarity of a well-focused heart and mind displays God's magnificent glory. The Scriptures provide the way to help us make corrections, to help us avoid a blurred existence and transform us to picture perfect—a picture of the Savior, that is.

## GETTING ACQUAINTED

### Just for Fun

Hobbies are activities we find enjoyable no matter what anyone else thinks: quilting, gardening, cooking, woodworking, racquetball, etc. They serve a very useful purpose, taking our minds off the stress of the day and focusing our attention elsewhere, usually on something we deeply desire to do. Let's look at our hobbies as examples of things that get our attention.

What is one thing you like to do "just for fun"? Why do you like doing this?

What kinds of accomplishments have you achieved in your pursuit of this hobby or interest?

How does this hobby or interest enhance your life?

For most of us, getting our eyes on our hobbies is not difficult. If life with Christ encompasses and lends meaning to everything we do—including our hobbies—what makes it difficult to "fix our eyes on Jesus"?

# GAINING INSIGHT

**Focusing on Jesus**
Read Hebrews 12:1-13.

¹Therefore, since we are surrounded by such a great cloud of witnesses, let us throw off everything that hinders and the sin that so easily entangles, and let us run with perseverance the race marked out for us. ²Let us fix our eyes on Jesus, the author and perfecter of our faith, who for the joy set before Him endured the cross, scorning its shame, and sat down at the right hand of the throne of God. ³Consider Him who endured such opposition from sinful men, so that you will not grow weary and lose heart.

⁴In your struggle against sin, you have not yet resisted to the point of shedding your blood. ⁵And you have forgotten that word of encouragement that addresses you as sons: My son, do not make light of the Lord's discipline, and do not lose heart when He rebukes you, ⁶because the Lord disciplines those He loves, and He punishes everyone He accepts as a son.

⁷Endure hardship as discipline; God is treating you as sons. For what son is not disciplined by his father? ⁸If you are not disciplined (and everyone undergoes discipline), then you are illegitimate children and not true sons. ⁹Moreover, we have all had human fathers who disciplined us and we respected them for it. How much more should we submit to the Father of our spirits and live! ¹⁰Our fathers disciplined us for a little while as they thought best; but God disciplines us for our good, that we may share in His holiness. ¹¹No discipline seems pleasant at the time, but painful. Later on, however, it produces a harvest of righteousness and peace for those who have been trained by it.

¹²Therefore, strengthen your feeble arms and weak knees. ¹³Make level paths for your feet, so that the lame may not be disabled but rather healed.

**Hebrews 12:1-13**

Hebrews 12:1 talks about throwing off everything that would

**25**

hinder us and the sin that so easily entangles us. It seems
that the author is dividing the obstacles to running the race
for Christ into two areas: (1) things that *hinder* us from running the race, which may not be characterized as sinful; (2)
other activities and attitudes that *restrict* us in the race, which
*could* be classified as sinful.

Take a few moments about your current level of energy and
effectiveness in the Christian "race." Fill in the columns below with entries that are true of your experience.

| Behaviors/Attitudes hindering my ability to run (not necessarily sinful) | Behaviors/Attitudes restricting my ability to run (sinful) |
|---|---|
| | |

When one runs a race there is usually a goal. In Hebrews
12:2 we have our goal marked out before us. What is that
goal?

Jesus is described for us in this passage not only in terms of
who He is but also in terms of what He has done. How are
Christ's character and actions described in Hebrews 12:2-3?

How can Jesus' example be encouraging to you as you go
through your struggles on this earth? (See Heb. 12:1, 3.)

What word is repeated so often in Hebrews 12:5-11?

Summarize the thought of these verses in your own words:

In order to think clearly about discipline and your experience with it, recall a scene from your childhood, a time when you were disciplined for something you did wrong. Imagine that you are at that age right now and make an entry in your diary:

Dear Diary ...

Name:
My age at the time of the incident:
What happened:

How I felt at the time:

How I feel about it now:

Think:
❑ What overall "message" did you get from your childhood experiences with discipline?

❑ What overall "message" comes through to you, from this passage, about God's discipline?

❏ How do the two "messages" compare and contrast in your mind today?


Being disciplined by a human parent is usually helpful but often imperfect. Yet it serves as an analogy to highlight the superiority of God's discipline. In Hebrews 12:9-10 this discipline is described in terms of the *result* following the discipline and the author writes of the quality and purpose of the discipline. What is:

The result of human discipline? (v. 9)


The result of the Father's discipline? (v. 9)


The quality of human discipline? (v. 10)


The quality and purpose of divine discipline? (v. 10)


God's disciplining hand in our lives has a result that is to be felt in the lives of others. In what ways should we see the impact of faithfully receiving the discipline of God, according to Hebrews 12:12-13?

 GROWING BY DOING

**"Hard" Things**
Is anyone in your group undergoing a particular trial or hardship? The only way we will know is to make sure the group is a safe place to share our deepest concerns with one another. Take time, first of all, to look at your own life and jot down a few "hard" things that are going on in your life right now.

Talk in groups of two or three about one "hard" thing you are encountering. Jot down what is shared by others so that you can more effectively pray for them during the week.

Ask each other if there is something you can do to alleviate this "hardship," or at least make it easier to bear. Write down ideas that you can do for the others.

If you have time, share with one another your responses to the two questions below. In what ways might the particular hardship I'm experiencing be related to ...

my need for better "focus"?

God's correcting ministry in my life?

## GOING THE SECOND MILE

**Thinking About the Group**

As a group, is there a project you could do that might be effective in "strengthening your feeble arms" so that "the lame ... may be healed"? Perhaps a group effort to volunteer at a food pantry or to help feed the homeless? Jot down some ways the group could be an agent of healing to those undergoing hardship:

### Thinking About Yourself

Most of us tolerate a certain amount of sin in our lives. Therefore, we are often encumbered by things that hinder us from running the race of the Christian life with full effectiveness.

Give some thought to why these things may continue to have a place in your life. What might be some reasons from your past, as a child growing up?

What needs do you have in your life now (perhaps related to those past events), that cry out for attention?

In what unhealthy or self-destructive ways have you sought to meet those needs?

What steps can you take, now, to focus greater attention on God's love and care for you—and His ability to meet your needs through the Author and Perfecter of your faith?

### Thinking About Your World

Can you think of someone outside of the group who may be undergoing a severe trial? Envision how you could share some aspect of the message of Hebrews 12:1-13 with them. How could you be an encouragement to that person? What could you do?

# THREE

*Lifestyle*

**GroupSpeak:** *"I know I'm supposed to be heavenly minded, but I need to know how to get to that point. In my group, I sometimes get the impression that everyone is living on this high plane of spiritual 'victory.' Is that really true? Or are we mostly 'faking it' "?*

**Rich, Famous and . . . Holy?**
A television show called "Lifestyles of the Rich and Famous" demonstrates what a wonderful lifestyle we would have if we had found fame and fortune. We are paraded through somebody's house to see all the exciting possessions the owner has accumulated because of his or her fantastic attainments. For most of the viewing audience this is the only chance to "live" the fantasy of "making it big" in show business and having the lifestyle to match. When the TV goes off, viewers are left to their own living rooms staring at worn furniture, with little hope of making it to Beverly Hills.

But Christians are to look at life from a heavenly perspective. We are to develop a way of life that is distinct from the world. We may never attain wealth and power, but we can attain a holy life. In fact, that wonderful goal is not an option for Christians. We must live our lives to a different standard. Paul, in Colossians 3:1-11, talks about this heavenly style of living in which our attitudes and actions flow from the reality that our lives are "hidden with Christ in God."

## GETTING ACQUAINTED

**The Typical Day**
"Check in" with the group by saying your name and telling how you are feeling at the moment. Then explain what you did this morning at 10 A.M. In what way is this a "typical" day for you?

Did you share anything in common with someone else in the group, as far as your lifestyle is concerned? Who was that person? In groups of two or three, compare and contrast: (1) typical days, (2) weekend activities, and (3) size of your immediate family.

How is your lifestyle dissimilar from the "lifestyles of the rich and famous"?

What is one aspect of your life that characterizes you as someone who desires to adopt the lifestyle of the Savior?

## GAINING INSIGHT

**A Heavenly Mind-Set**
Read Colossians 3:1-11.

**¹Since, then, you have been raised with Christ, set your hearts on things above, where Christ is seated at the right hand of God. ²Set your minds on things above, not on earthly things. ³For you died, and your life is hidden with Christ in God. ⁴When Christ, who is your life, appears, then you also will appear with Him in glory.**

**34**

⁵Put to death, therefore, whatever belongs to your earthly nature: sexual immorality, impurity, lust, evil desires, and greed, which is idolatry. ⁶Because of these, the wrath of God is coming. ⁷You used to walk in these ways, in the life you once lived. ⁸But now you must rid yourselves of all such things as these: anger, rage, malice, slander, and filthy language from your lips. ⁹Do not lie to each other, since you have taken off your old self with its practices ¹⁰and have put on the new self, which is being renewed in knowledge of the Creator. ¹¹Here there is no Greek or Jew, circumcised or uncircumcised, barbarian, Scythian, slave or free, but Christ is all, and is in all.

**Colossians 3:1-11**

It is obvious that we are to live lives that are different from many of those in our world. For instance, in a day when "safe sex" is the moral standard, God gives different guidelines for our relationships. Those guidelines will not be very popular on TV, but then God's audience here is not the world, but the believer: You and me. The world may not understand, but we must understand these things.

What are some of the "earthly things" that dominate your thinking?

When Paul says to set our minds on things above, he is urging us to have the view from heaven as we encounter issues and decisions in our lives. We look at these from Christ's exalted standpoint. How would such a perspective affect:

❑ the relationships you have with your loved ones?

❑ your approach to frustrations at home or on the job?

❑ your response to the sickness or death of a friend?

**35**

❑ your decisions about how to use your money?

Notice that the apostle says "you died" (v. 3); therefore, "put to death" (v. 5) certain things. In what way are you "dead" and in what way are you apparently *not* dead?

In Colossians 3:5 we find a list of certain behaviors that Paul urges us to put to death. What would most people in your world of influence say if you urged this "inner assassination project" on them?

What is your immediate reaction to the practicality of Paul's commands here?

Did you notice that greed is equated with idolatry? Why would this be? Give an example of a way you have seen this equation verified in real life.

Colossians 3:8 gives us more behaviors to remove from our lives. This time, though, the focus is on relationships with others. Choose two of these behaviors and give examples of when you have seen them demonstrated—by yourself or by others. Offer suggestions on how the people involved *should* have acted.

1.

2.

When Paul says, "Do not lie to each other," he is speaking to believers in the church. In what ways do Christians lie to each other?

How could Christians, in groups like ours, start being more honest and open with one another?

Paul says that the new self is being "renewed in knowledge" of the Creator, of God in Christ. Here are some of the attributes of God that we can acquire through our walk with Christ. (Note: omnipotence, omnipresence and omniscience are not possible for us, but other godly attributes can be built into our lives.) Pick at least two of the godly attributes below and jot down an example of how those qualities could be displayed in a practical situation within your daily routine. Be prepared to share these with your group.

❏ **Loving**

❏ **Merciful**

❏ **Just**

❏ **Patient**

❏ **Good**

❏ **Faithful**

One of the saddest statistics is that Christians experience divorce at a rate about the same as non-Christians. The bulk of these cases are tragic examples of two people who simply have refused to live according to the heavenly perspective we've been considering. They have allowed their lives to become significantly saturated with the world's standards. Having studied these standards, let us make a new commitment to refuse to live by anything other than God's desires.

 ## GROWING BY DOING

To what extent would you say your present attitudes and actions exhibit the mind-set of heaven? How would you mark these areas of your life on a scale of 1 to 10? What events, relationships, or attitudes serve as key illustrations of where you are?

| *Heavenly Mind-set* | | | | | | | | *Earthly Mind-set* | |
|---|---|---|---|---|---|---|---|---|---|

**Thought Life**
| 1 | 2 | 3 | 4 | 5 | 6 | 7 | 8 | 9 | 10 |
|---|---|---|---|---|---|---|---|---|---|

Key illustration:

**Work Life**
| 1 | 2 | 3 | 4 | 5 | 6 | 7 | 8 | 9 | 10 |
|---|---|---|---|---|---|---|---|---|---|

Key illustration:

**Family Life**
| 1 | 2 | 3 | 4 | 5 | 6 | 7 | 8 | 9 | 10 |
|---|---|---|---|---|---|---|---|---|---|

Key illustration:

**Church Life**
| 1 | 2 | 3 | 4 | 5 | 6 | 7 | 8 | 9 | 10 |
|---|---|---|---|---|---|---|---|---|---|

Key illustration:

*Heavenly Mind-set*                    *Earthly Mind-set*

    1    2    3    4    5    6    7    8    9    10

**Overall Goals and Priorities**

Key illustration:

Summary statement about the extent of the "Heaven Factor" at work in my lifestyle right now:

In groups of three or four answer the following: What will characterize your thinking in the next week? What positive steps could you make to change your lifestyle (at least in one small way) to make it more attuned to Christ's standards?

## GOING THE SECOND MILE

**Thinking About the Group**
Encourage someone in the group through a comment, prayer, or note about how they can be a person characterized by a kingdom lifestyle. Write out what you will do.

**Thinking About Yourself**
Is there something you need to confess before God or with another person that has become a barrier to your relationship? Will you follow through and do this?

**Thinking About Your World**
Write a prayer for those who have to deal with a world dedicated to ungodly behaviors. Include politicians, police, and counselors, among others, in your prayer.

# FOUR

*Relationships*

**GroupSpeak:** *"I've found that working on my relationships with other Christians is well worth my time and effort. The greatest thing is seeing the unity of the Holy Spirit spilling over into everyday interactions."*

**True Harmony: Is It Possible?**

*Harmony.* Isn't it a great word? There is something so peaceful in the concept. When singers or musicians are in harmony there is order and a strange sort of power. The message gets across. When a football team is playing in harmony, the goal of winning the game is much more attainable. Each part blends with the other to produce impact. But the question remains: Is harmony really possible among Christians?

Surely all Christians want harmony. Some desire it so much that they avoid conflict at all costs. Others want it only on their own terms. They produce conflict to get their way.

God desires harmony as well. But there are principles we can build into our lives so that the harmony produced is a healthy, edifying harmony. In this session we will look at these principles to help us get in tune with God's expectations for healthy, holy relationships.

## GETTING ACQUAINTED

**Getting Along**

If you don't already know each other in the group, or, if there is a newcomer, introduce yourself to the others. Then, tell about a friend or relative with whom you get along very well. Who is this person and what is he or she like?

What makes your relationship with that person so strong and satisfying?

Think of a relationship that is strained. What characteristics of that relationship make it difficult?

Before launching into the rest of this study, list some principles that you believe would contribute to great harmony in relationships.

## GAINING INSIGHT

**Oriented to Others**

Read Romans 12:10; 15:7; 16:16 and Hebrews 10:24-25 aloud.

¹⁰**Be devoted to one another in brotherly love. Honor one another above yourselves.**

**Romans 12:10**

⁷**Accept one another, then, just as Christ accepted you, in order to bring praise to God.**

**Romans 15:7**

¹⁶**Greet one another with a holy kiss. All the churches of Christ send greetings.**

**Romans 16:16**

**²⁴And let us consider how we may spur one another on toward love and good deeds. ²⁵Let us not give up meeting together, as some are in the habit of doing, but let us encourage one another—and all the more as you see the Day approaching.**

**Hebrews 10:24-25**

What two key words are repeated in each of these verses?

These verses can transform your group—even your life—if you put them into practice. If you will concentrate on actively making these commands the guiding principles of your group, you will not be able to contain the sense of harmony and goodwill that will blossom among you. Others will want to be a part of it.

What is the command of Romans 12:10?

In what ways could we *do* this in our group? Be very specific. These must be practical things you could plan on doing now or next week.

What makes these things difficult to do in our culture?

What is the command of Romans 15:7?

In what ways could we *do* this in our group? Again be very specific.

What makes these things difficult to do in our culture?

What is the command of Romans 16:16?

In what ways could we *do* this in our group?

What makes these things difficult to do in our culture?

What are the three commands of Hebrews 10:24-25?

Picking one of these commands, in what ways could we *do* this in our group? Be very specific.

What makes these things difficult to do in our culture?

We have only looked at five verses, but let's not minimize the impact these can have on us. We can look at our personal interactions with those close to us, both in the group and at home, to see how we can improve those relationships. Then we can look around us at how we deal with strangers to apply these principles to all relationships.

### Case Studies in Relating
Choose a partner and pick one of the situations below to discuss together. Your tasks during the discussion time are:

(a) choose the Bible passage that seems most closely applicable to the situation as a principle upon which to base a possible resolution of the problem; (b) decide what "first steps" should be taken by each individual in the situation; (c) share with your partner a related incident from your own experience. Tell what happened and give your insights about the situation today.

Be prepared to share with the whole group aspects of your discussion under points a and b.

**Situation #1:** Robert secretly dreaded the invitation to the Smith's house for an evening Bible study group. Because the Smith's had a huge, beautiful house, Robert knew he would feel ashamed of the small apartment he and his wife, Sue, were providing for their family.

As soon as Ken Smith answered the door, he said: "Welcome, Robert, to our little palace!" Robert felt his face grow hot and red, but decided to say nothing. He was very quiet during the rest of the evening....

**Situation #2:** Akeem wanted his study group to meet his deep needs for fellowship and personal sharing. His vision was to be in a group where just about any personal problem or struggle could be raised and dealt with through prayer and loving support. But during the last few weeks, Don, a new person in the group, has seemed to dominate the atmosphere. Don is considered a very committed Christian who regularly urges the other group members to be more faithful in personal evangelism. Don has won three people to Christ in the last month.

Akeem appreciates Don's gift, but wonders what happened to the group as his place of "spiritual tank-filling." He's thinking of dropping out of the group....

**Situation #3:** For years Marty had thought his pastor was just *great*. In fact, after some sermons, Marty felt so encouraged and inspired that he couldn't wait until the next Sunday's preaching service. When the pastor suddenly resigned from the church, under suspicion of improper behavior, Marty was crushed. He had no idea where to turn for the kind of inspiration he had become so used to. His spiritual life began to shrivel and dry up.

But the straw that broke the camel's back was an incident on the last Sunday Marty attended church, three months ago. Chris had walked up to him and said: "How about that pastor! I always knew he was less of a saint than he pretended to be!"

**Situation #4:** Shelly longs to experience the care of other Christians. She's made friends with several friendly people in her Bible study group, but she also senses a fear of touch among the members. Once Shelly felt moved to give Jane a hug after a time of meaningful prayer. Jane seemed to freeze up and said, "I'll go make some coffee for everybody."

Shelly knows that a big part of her spiritual and personal growth involves overcoming an extreme lack of parental affection in her childhood. But she wonders whether a church group could, or should, supply some of the human warmth she knows she needs. She's thinking of supplementing her Bible study with a dance class on another night....

## GROWING BY DOING

As a group, compose a list of guidelines for relating in your small group based on the principles you discern in this lesson's Bible passages. Do not simply restate the commands but think of how they could apply in group life. For instance, you could formulate a guideline on how to encourage one another, such as: We will take time to listen to what people are involved in and pray for them as a means of encouraging them.

Guideline One:

Guideline Two:

Guideline Three:

Guideline Four:

Guideline Five:

In groups of three or four answer the following: Pick two of the guidelines above and discuss with each other how you could employ them in your group, close relationships, or in your relationships with others outside of the group.

## GOING THE SECOND MILE

**Thinking About the Group**
What could you personally do to employ one of these guidelines in your group the next time you get together?

**Thinking About Yourself**
What is your most needy or unharmonious relationship? What can you do to employ these guidelines in that relationship? What obstacles do you envision hindering you?

**Thinking About Your World**
As you consider your world of influence, can you think of a relationship that would be improved through practicing one or more of these guidelines? What is that relationship and which guidelines could you employ? Jot some notes about the special needs of this relationship, and then spend some time in prayer about it.

# FIVE

## *Partnership*

**GroupSpeak:** *"I never realized before that I'm a 'gifted' person! But, according to the Bible, I have been given a special ability — a spiritual gift — to help our church stay healthy and growing."*

### Doing the Work Together

Have you ever watched an experienced mason at work, as he carefully fashions a wall with bricks, mortar, trowel, and sheer muscle? One marvels that all the lines end up straight, the wall does not bow, there are no cracks. The wall is strong, able to fulfill its purpose as an integral part of the building.

The mason knows that he does not work alone; he is in partnership. He relies upon the brickyard to make bricks of quality to build with. He depends upon the truck driver to deliver them. He counts on his helper to mix the mortar and bring more bricks. And, of course, he needs a contractor to keep the jobs coming in an orderly fashion. It is true the mason could, perhaps, do all these things alone. But this would waste his valuable expertise as a mason.

Consider a similar picture of partnership in the church: God has granted gifts so that we all can participate in building God's church. Partnership is vital here, too. We cannot do it

**49**

alone. It is God's plan that we recognize the gifts He has given us, valuable gifts, talents, and abilities to accomplish the work of mutual edification of believers and outreach to seekers.

## GETTING ACQUAINTED

### Doing Things Well

What is one thing you do very well and enjoy doing? What makes it an enjoyable thing to do?

What do you *not* do well that you wish you could do? Why?

From what was shared in the group, have you noticed anything you have in common with someone, or something that you admire in another person? Jot it down.

## GAINING INSIGHT

### Life in the Body of Christ
Read 1 Corinthians 12:1-27.

¹Now about spiritual gifts, brothers, I do not want you to be ignorant. ²You know that when you were pagans, somehow or other you were influenced and led astray to dumb idols. ³Therefore I tell you that no one who is speaking by the Spirit of God says, "Jesus be cursed," and no one can say, "Jesus is Lord," except by the Holy Spirit.

⁴There are different kinds of gifts, but the same Spirit. ⁵There are different kinds of service, but the same Lord. ⁶There are different kinds of working, but the same God works all of them in all men.

**50**

⁷Now to each one the manifestation of the Spirit is given for the common good. ⁸To one there is given through the Spirit the message of wisdom, to another the message of knowledge by means of the same Spirit, ⁹to another faith by the same Spirit, to another gifts of healing by that one Spirit, ¹⁰to another miraculous powers, to another prophecy, to another the ability to distinguish between spirits, to another the ability to speak in different kinds of tongues, and to still another the interpretation of tongues. ¹¹All these are the work of one and the same Spirit, and He gives them to each one, just as He determines.

¹²The body is a unit, though it is made up of many parts; and though all its parts are many, they form one body. So it is with Christ. ¹³For we were all baptized by one Spirit into one body whether Jews or Greeks, slave or free—and we were all given the one Spirit to drink.

¹⁴Now the body is not made up of one part but of many. ¹⁵If the foot should say, "Because I am not a hand, I do not belong to the body," it would not for that reason cease to be part of the body. ¹⁶And if the ear should say, "Because I am not an eye, I do not belong to the body," it would not for that reason cease to be part of the body. ¹⁷If the whole body were an eye, where would the sense of hearing be? If the whole body were an ear, where would the sense of smell be? ¹⁸But in fact God has arranged the parts in the body, every one of them, just as He wanted them to be. ¹⁹If they were all one part, where would the body be? ²⁰As it is, there are many parts, but one body.

²¹The eye cannot say to the hand, "I don't need you!" And the head cannot say to the feet, "I don't need you!" ²²On the contrary, those parts of the body that seem to be weaker are indispensable, ²³and the parts that we think are less honorable we treat with special honor. And the parts that are unpresentable are treated with special modesty, ²⁴while our presentable parts need no special treatment. But God has combined the members of the body and has given greater honor to the parts that lacked it, ²⁵so that there should be no division in the body, but that its parts should have equal concern for each other.

²⁶**If one part suffers, every part suffers with it; if one part is honored, every part rejoices with it.**

²⁷**Now you are the body of Christ and each one of you is a part of it.**

**1 Corinthians 12:1-27**

What is Paul's desire regarding spiritual gifts, according to 1 Corinthians 12:1?

What words are repeated in 1 Corinthians 12:4-6? What message does this communicate to you? How would you state the important principle here in your own words?

Who selects the gifts we are to have for ourselves, according to 1 Corinthians 12:11? What difference does this make as we look at how we have been gifted?

The section of this chapter from 12:7-26 can be divided into three parts. Summarize each section by paraphrasing it in your own words.

1 Corinthians 12:7-13

1 Corinthians 12:14-20

1 Corinthians 12:21-26

What implication does Paul wish to draw from 1 Corinthians 12:27?

Discuss: How can we hold a sense of unity in the church

**52**

while affirming our diversity? What are some areas of Bible interpretation, or preferences in church ministry style or methods, in which we can celebrate our diversity?

One fact is indisputable: We are the body of Christ. We must develop a sense of partnership to make the body work as it ought.

How would you explain these crucial points to someone who wanted to know more about the proper functioning of the church? Imagine you are a pastor planning to preach a sermon on 1 Corinthians 12:1-27, or on some portion of the passage. (Focus on any particular portion of the passage you feel speaks to you most powerfully.) What key things would you want to say to your congregation about "partnership" from this passage? Make the sermon as practical and applicable to everyday life as possible.

Take a few moments to skim the passage again and jot down a sermon outline and notes that include the following:

Title:

Overall Theme Sentence:

The Main Points I'd Make:

Practical Application Suggestions:

Personal Illustration:

Conclusion Statement:

Consider sharing with the rest of the group about how you structured your sermon. Be sure to tell what key truths you would want to stress from this passage.

## GROWING BY DOING

People need assurance that they are valuable. Compile a list of people who you know work hard in your church and indicate what role they play. Of course, from your study in 1 Corinthians 12:1-27, you know that all Christians are important and have gifts to use in the body of Christ. But sometimes we need encouragement. From the list of people and their roles, distribute the names among your group members and write thank you notes acknowledging their partnership in the Gospel.

Pray specifically for those actively using their gifts. Write out a brief prayer for them in preparation for praying aloud in the group.

## GOING THE SECOND MILE

**Thinking About the Group**
What gifts are evident in your group? How can you acknowledge these gifts and encourage them?

Spend some time focusing on each group member, as others say to him or her: "I believe I have observed the gift of _____ in you, because of...."

**Thinking About Yourself**
In what ways are you gifted, talented, and able to serve either in your study group or in the larger church? Take a moment to silently think through this partial listing of gifts. Then jot down your insights about your ministry (or potential ministry) among other believers.

### Some Spiritual Gifts Listed in the New Testament
(1 Corinthians 12; Romans 12; 1 Peter 4)

❑ **Apostleship**—ability to be a "sent one" with the Gospel; missionary endeavor.

❑ **Teaching**—ability to communicate God's truths in powerful, life-changing ways.

❑ **Knowledge**—ability to perceive and organize the great facts of Scripture.

❑ **Wisdom**—ability to apply biblical insights to specific situations.

❑ **Faith**—a visionary outlook; ability to trust God in "impossible" situations.

❑ **Healing**—ability to foster wholeness in others: physical, emotional, spiritual; counseling.

❑ **Miracles**—ability through prayer to call on God to bypass laws of nature; seen in certain "Bible heroes."

❑ **Tongues and Interpretation of Tongues**—controversial, likely the ability to speak the Gospel in a foreign (or unknown) language; the ability to praise God for His mighty works.

❑ **Prophecy**—ability to preach effectively; able to encourage, console, warn.

☐ **Discernment of Spirits**—ability to distinguish between truth and error (usually in doctrine).

☐ **Helps, or the Gift of Serving**—ability to lend a hand where needed; works "behind the scenes."

☐ **Exhorting**—ability to counsel, comfort, console; encourages those who are spiritually faltering.

☐ **Giving**—ability to give sacrificially, yet joyfully.

☐ **Showing Mercy**—ability to empathize with those in hardship, and take action to help; often works with those who are despised or looked down on by others.

Areas of giftedness or expertise I am aware of:

How I have apparently used one or more of these strengths, with spiritual results, in the past:

My thoughts about my present/future areas of ministry in the church:

**Thinking About Your World**
Remember the list of people who are making a contribution in your church? It is one thing to write a note as a group to some of these people, it is even better to make affirmation and encouragement a regular part of our lives. How could you more fully develop this attitude in your life?

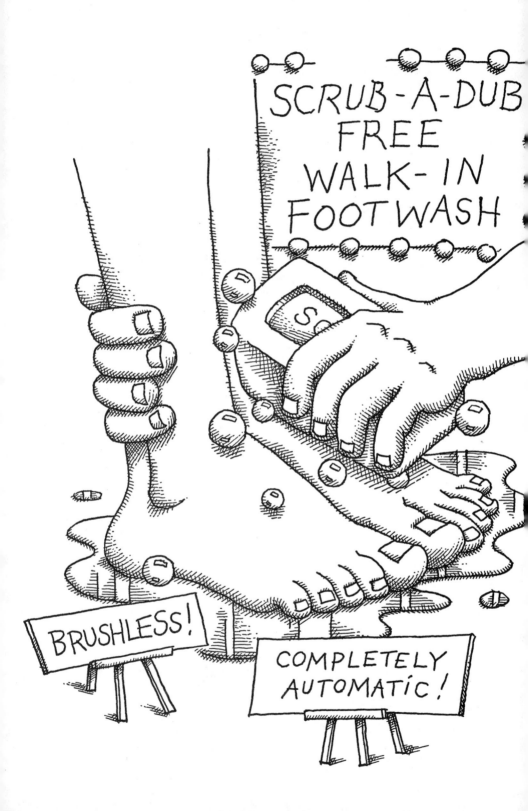

# SIX

## Service

**GroupSpeak:** *"I used to hear a lot about going into 'full-time Christian service' when I was a teen; that was considered the ultimate in discipleship. I'm glad the emphasis seems to have changed a bit: I'm a full-time Christian no matter what I'm doing! I guess that means I'm called to have a servant attitude twenty-four hours a day."*

### Divine Service

Dr. Alan Redpath, a former minister at Moody Church in Chicago, once told of a woman in the church who had a little motto posted on a plaque over her kitchen sink. The plaque read: "Divine service conducted here three times daily."

It's hard to find that kind of a servant in our day, though people in power are not hard to find. Some make it a point to remind you that they, indeed, are in power, and you are not. But no matter what role you play in life, "you got to serve somebody" (in the words of a popular song by Bob Dylan). What is remarkable, however, is to see people in positions of power serving those under them. They may be executives in large corporations or managers of small stores. If they use their influence to help those under them, not satisfied with simply enforcing the so-common "I'm in charge and don't you forget it" attitude, they stand out as a rare breed.

**59**

The attitude of a servant is not popular. But, then again, neither are the principles for our life-styles and relationships that we have been studying in these lessons. Christian servants are not to be about their own business, but about their Lord's business. Or perhaps we could say that as the Christian servant grows, he or she becomes less and less able to distinguish the two: his or her business, finally, *is* the Lord's business, no matter what the daily routine! This is another attitude-transforming step for the disciple who is sold out in devotion to Jesus.

## GETTING ACQUAINTED

### Tops in Service

We can all recall things that have served us well. Perhaps we have had a car, refrigerator, lawn mower, or other gadget that has simply done its job as we have asked. What are the things that qualify in this category for you, and why do they rank so high? What characteristics do you value in ranking this item high in the service category?

Can you think of people who may be in this category? What characteristics do you value in these people—people who serve well?

Whom do you serve? What qualities do you think you offer in being a servant?

As a group, list the overall qualities of a good servant:

# GAINING INSIGHT

**An Attitude Like Jesus!**
Read Philippians 2:1-11.

¹**If you have any encouragement from being united with Christ, if any comfort from His love, if any fellowship with the Spirit, if any tenderness and compassion, ²then make my joy complete by being like-minded, having the same love, being one in spirit and purpose. ³Do nothing out of selfish ambition or vain conceit, but in humility consider others better than yourselves. ⁴Each of you should look not only to your own interests, but also to the interests of others.**

⁵**Your attitude should be the same as that of Christ Jesus: ⁶Who, being in very nature God, did not consider equality with God something to be grasped, ⁷but made Himself nothing, taking the very nature of a servant, being made in human likeness. ⁸And being found in appearance as a man He humbled Himself and became obedient to death—even death on a cross! ⁹Therefore God exalted Him to the highest place and gave Him the name that is above every name, ¹⁰that at the name of Jesus every knee should bow, in heaven and on earth and under the earth, ¹¹and every tongue confess that Jesus Christ is Lord, to the glory of God the Father.**

**Philippians 2:1-11**

From the text above it is obvious that Jesus is the consummate servant. We can, indeed must, look to Him as the example for strengthening the attitude of servanthood in our own lives. Service does not mean we will be wimpy, simply acquiescing to other people's views as "human doormats." Quite the contrary: We make a principled decision to serve others for their ultimate good because we have been called by our Lord to do so. This may please others, and it may not. But regardless, it is our service mandate from Jesus.

Paul, in effect, asks us whether we have received anything in Christ in Philippians 2:1. Our "yes" to these questions should lead us on to different attitudes and actions. In what way do you have:

**61**

❏ encouragement from being united with Christ in salvation?

❏ comfort from His love (that is, a sense of his tender care)?

❏ fellowship with the Spirit (that is, a sense of God's presence and empowering)?

What are the two commands given in Philippians 2:3?

Summarize the dual command of Philippians 2:4.

In what ways does Jesus keep these commands, as described in Philippians 2:6-8?

What was the Father's response to Christ's actions? What lesson do you, personally, draw from this for your everyday life?

What are the principles that a servant is to follow according to this passage?

Although Philippians 2:6-11 was not written for the purpose of giving us a complete doctrinal understanding of who Christ is, we do learn a lot about Him from these verses. Explain what we learn of the nature of Christ.

In an age in which people are more into self-service than the service of others, we are challenged by these words of Paul. Actions, of course, enable us to cement a servant attitude into our character. We should not wait until we "feel" like becoming a servant. (We probably would never naturally feel like it.) But we can at least "act" the part, at first. Here's an exercise that can help you envision what true Christian servanthood looks like in real life.

Imagine finding a Help Wanted ad like this: **Wanted: A servant to serve others sacrificially in the kingdom. Salary unpredictable, long hours, but excellent benefits and (very) long-term pension plan. Also prophet/sharing program. Apply directly to Mr. J.C.**

Suppose an excellent Christian servant were to apply. What would that person's resume look like? Fill in the blanks below to indicate your vision of realistic Christian servanthood.

**RESUMÉ**
for
**AN EXCELLENT CHRISTIAN SERVANT**

*Primary Qualifications*
❏ Heart

❏ Soul

❏ Mind

❏ Body

*Experience*
❏ with the joy of helping others grow in Christ

❏ with discouragement and lack of recognition

❏ with submitting to God's will

❏ with humility and perseverance

❏ with prayer, worship, and meditation on the Word

*Key Accomplishments*
❏ Church

❏ Home

❏ Community

## GROWING BY DOING

A group service project would reinforce the servant attitude we've studied. Brainstorm how your group can act in an other-serving sort of way. The only guidelines you should keep in mind are: (1) the project should not serve the group itself; (2) it should be explicitly in the name of Christ; and (3) it should simply serve other people, calling attention, not to your great skill, but to your faithful Lord. List some of your ideas below.

From the list above, select the area of service that would be most appropriate and designate people to research and plan the service project:

After the service project is over answer the following questions:

What did you "get" from your service?

Did this action have benefits for you personally? as a group?

What criteria would you use to determine the "success" of a service project carried out in Christ's name?

## GOING THE SECOND MILE

**Thinking About the Group**
To further embed these principles in your character, think of someone you can serve from the group. What could you do for that person during the coming year?

**Thinking About Yourself**
Do a personal attitude check based on Philippians 2:1-5. In what ways would you like to change your thinking and actions toward other people?

What is the first step for you to take in initiating that change?

**Thinking About Your World**
Politicians are to serve their constituents. Write a prayer for one of your elected officials. You may even choose to send it to that person for his or her encouragement.

# SEVEN

## Possessions

**GroupSpeak:** *"I can get pretty worried about money. In fact, because I grew up in a home that really struggled financially, my tendency is to look to my bank account as a primary source of security. I know that sounds terrible, but what can I do?"*

### Imagine No Commercials!

Can you imagine a world with no advertising? We would drive down highways with no billboards, watch TV with no commercials, and have newspapers of one-third the size. And we would never have heard of "ring around the collar!"

Advertisers spend millions of dollars researching the best ways to convince the public to buy what they represent. Then they spend billions to present it to us, doing their best to get us to stick our hands in our pockets and shell out the money. They certainly are successful! Like the three year old who asserts, "I want it," without even waiting for the answer to "What is it?" we scarcely know what a product is before the advertiser has us thinking we really could use it!

In the midst of such advertising mania, how are we going to "get a handle" on our urge to get a handle on *things!* The disciple of Jesus must look to the Master to gain what he or she needs to combat this contagious disease. We need to heed the teachings of the Master Himself. In so doing we will store up for ourselves eternal treasures in heaven.

## GETTING ACQUAINTED

### What Is It? I Want It!

What products are being advertised today with magnificent effectiveness? What messages do the advertisers want to project about these certain products? How truthful are they? Do we really *need* these products?

Describe, without any exaggeration, some utensil or item in your household that you really do highly value:

Describe, as an aggressive salesperson would, another item, but this time an item which is not very important to you:

How do we scrutinize our viewing and hearing of these advertisements to win the war over the acquisition of unnecessary things?

## GAINING INSIGHT

Read Luke 12:13-34.

**[13]Someone in the crowd said to Him, "Teacher, tell my brother to divide the inheritance with me." [14]Jesus replied, "Man, who appointed Me a judge or an arbiter between you?" [15]Then He said to them, "Watch out! Be on your**

guard against all kinds of greed; a man's life does not consist in the abundance of his possessions."

¹⁶And He told them this parable: "The ground of a certain rich man produced a good crop. ¹⁷He thought to himself, 'What shall I do? I have no place to store my crops.'

¹⁸"Then he said, 'This is what I'll do. I will tear down my barns and build bigger ones, and there I will store all my grain and my goods. ¹⁹And I'll say to myself, You have plenty of good things laid up for many years. Take life easy; eat, drink and be merry.'

²⁰"But God said to him, 'You fool! This very night your life will be demanded from you. Then who will get what you have prepared for yourself?'

²¹"This is how it will be with anyone who stores up things for himself but is not rich toward God."

²²Then Jesus said to His disciples: "Therefore I tell you, do not worry about your life, what you will eat; or about your body, what you will wear. ²³Life is more than food, and the body more than clothes. ²⁴Consider the ravens: They do not sow or reap, they have no storeroom or barn; yet God feeds them. And how much more valuable you are than birds! ²⁵Who of you by worrying can add a single hour to his life? ²⁶Since you cannot do this very little thing, why do you worry about the rest?

²⁷Consider how the lilies grow. They do not labor or spin. Yet I tell you, not even Solomon in all his splendor was dressed like one of these. ²⁸If that is how God clothes the grass of the field, which is here today and tomorrow is thrown into the fire, how much more will He clothe you, O you of little faith! ²⁹And do not set your heart on what you will eat or drink; do not worry about it. ³⁰For the pagan world runs after all such things, and your Father knows that you need them. ³¹But seek His kingdom, and these things will be given to you as well.

³²Do not be afraid, little flock, for your Father has been

**pleased to give you the kingdom. ³³Sell your possessions and give to the poor. Provide purses for yourselves that will not wear out, a treasure in heaven that will not be exhausted, where no thief comes near and no moth destroys. ³⁴For where your treasure is, there your heart will be also.**

**Luke 12:13-34**

Western society is a consumer society. The words of Jesus simply don't compute very well here. For us, happiness is the sound of a ringing cash register just before we take home our long-anticipated purchase. So these words of Jesus are a necessary antidote to what ails our society. Will we allow them to influence us toward a more godly view of possessions?

Jesus uses a confrontation between brothers to warn the disciples against the perils of greed. The principle He wishes to get across is given in Luke 12:15. The principle is:

A man's life

The parable Jesus told in Luke 12:16-21 illustrates this principle. What is the attitude of the rich according to Luke 12:18-19?

What is the problem the rich man did not anticipate?

How does Luke 12:21 reinforce the point of Luke 12:15?

On the positive side, Jesus teaches His disciples about how to have a proper viewpoint regarding the necessities of life. What do His words about the ravens teach us?

What do His words about the lilies teach us?

The pagan who does not follow God cannot claim which truth, given in Luke 12:30?

What should the disciple do, according to Luke 12:31?

Preparing treasures in heaven requires what actions and attitudes? What will be the result?

This teaching should help jar us out of our preoccupation with possessions. With the help and encouragement of fellow brothers and sisters in Christ, we may, indeed, be able to fight off the tendency to be attached to things.

As you consider what you have studied in this section, how would you characterize your current level of worry about money and/or possessions? Mark one of the sentence completions below to indicate your overall attitude.

"I'd have to say that, when it comes to money, I'm most like . . .

❏ a squabbling brother
❏ a gung-ho barn builder
❏ a nervous raven
❏ a peaceful lily

Share your response with the rest of the group and clarify it with a personal example.

## GROWING BY DOING

Here is a wild thought: Let's sell some of our possessions and give the money to the poor! Should we? Is it a "reasonable" suggestion that a group target some of its possessions for giving away? Wouldn't this be a dramatic statement to our friends, to our relatives, to our family, to ourselves, and to our Lord that we refuse to be attached to things? Discuss the merits of this suggestion. Jot your notes here:

**Pros**                                                  **Cons**

If the above suggestion does *not* seem reasonable, perhaps the group should target a date when the group will take up a collection and give money specifically to the poor. Brainstorm some possibilities here. Jot down the first five ideas that come to mind, and be prepared to share them with the rest of the group.

In groups of three or four answer the following: What worries do I have about security, money, or possessions that I wish I could let go of and approach with greater faith?

## GOING THE SECOND MILE

**Thinking About the Group**

From the small group exercise above, jot down the name of a person and need for which you can pray in the next days:

**Thinking About Yourself**
Being brutally honest with yourself, consider how much you are tied to possessions. Write a brief prayer of confession to Jesus regarding your past attitudes:

**Thinking About Your World**
Who are the "poor" in your part of the world? How could you make a small impact on their lives with your new-found perspective on "things." What will you do?

# EIGHT

## *Continuing in the Faith*

**GroupSpeak:** *"It'd be nice, wouldn't it, just to go up on a hill somewhere and wait for Jesus to come back? But the Apostle Paul says we've got to 'hold the fort' until that day."*

### Final Instructions

Imagine you are the Apostle Paul at the end of your life. You are looking over what was accomplished. You certainly have made an impact on the world. But you are aware that what was done was only by the grace of God. And you are convinced that the work must be carried on by others. The Day of Christ's return has not yet occurred. Therefore it is time to give instructions to those who will continue working diligently to spread the Gospel and build the church.

This is the situation confronting Paul as he writes Timothy. (We learn so much about being a disciple through looking at Paul and Timothy.) As we look at the challenge of continuing in the faith, we can be confident that God is able to guard what we have entrusted to Him. Until we see Him face-to-face we must rest in Christ's strength, power, and love.

## GETTING ACQUAINTED

**A Review**

Look back through this book. Take note of the lessons you have learned. Which ones seemed to have had the most impact on your life? Why?

Which lessons do you think had greatest impact on the group? Why?

Is there any evidence of significant spiritual growth in your life that you would like to share with the group?

Is there a lesson you think would be good to review in a future session? Which one and why?

## GAINING INSIGHT

**Not Ashamed**
Read 2 Timothy 1:3-14.

³I thank God, whom I serve, as my forefathers did, with a clear conscience, as night and day I constantly remember you in my prayers. ⁴Recalling your tears, I long to see you, so that I may be filled with joy. ⁵I have been reminded of your sincere faith, which first lived in your grandmother Lois and in your mother Eunice and, I am persuaded, now lives in you also. ⁶For this reason I remind you to fan into flame the gift of God, which is in you through the laying on of my hands. ⁷For God did not give

us a spirit of timidity, but a spirit of power, of love and of self-discipline.

⁸So do not be ashamed to testify about our Lord, or ashamed of me His prisoner. But join with me in suffering for the Gospel, by the power of God, ⁹who has saved us and called us to a holy life—not because of anything we have done but because of his own purpose and grace. This grace was given us in Christ Jesus before the beginning of time, ¹⁰but it has now been revealed through the appearing of our Savior, Christ Jesus, who has destroyed death and has brought life and immortality to light through the Gospel. ¹¹And of this Gospel I was appointed a herald and an apostle and a teacher. ¹²That is why I am suffering as I am. Yet I am not ashamed, because I know whom I have believed, and am convinced that He is able to guard what I have entrusted to Him for that day.

¹³What you heard from me, keep as the pattern of sound teaching, with faith and love in Christ Jesus. ¹⁴Guard the good deposit that was entrusted to you—guard it with the help of the Holy Spirit who lives in us.

**2 Timothy 1:3-14**

These words from Paul's pen were divinely inspired for us as well as Timothy. As we close off this series of lessons, let us commit afresh to following after Christ without looking back.

Paul, near the end of his life, writes some reminders to Timothy. What are the personal characteristics of Timothy and Paul, as revealed in 2 Timothy 1:3-6?

❏ Characteristics of Timothy

❏ Characteristics of Paul

Paul admonished Timothy to "fan into flame the gift of God" (v. 6). What did Paul mean?

What does this injunction mean to you, personally?

Paul linked this command with what reason, according to 2 Timothy 1:7?

What command is given in 2 Timothy 1:8? Why is the spirit of power, love, and self-discipline important to carrying this out?

❑ Power

❑ Love

❑ Self-control

How is the power of God evident? (See 2 Timothy 1:9-11.)

What does Paul rest on now that he is at the end of his life? (v. 12) Why is this now important?

Timothy received sound teaching from Paul, according to 2 Timothy 1:13. How are we to acquire the same type of teaching?

## GROWING BY DOING

How can your group as a whole carry out the command Paul gave to Timothy in 2 Timothy 1:8? Who are you actively pursuing with the purpose of sharing the Gospel? Which of the three—power, love, or self-discipline do you most need? What support do you need from the group to add more power, love, or self-discipline to your life?

What is the next step the group can take to obtain more teachings from God, just as Paul urged Timothy to keep the sound teaching? Make plans now to move on in learning more from the Scriptures.

Will you continue to pursue these goals as a group? If so, agree on your next meeting time and pray for your group's continued growth.

## GOING THE SECOND MILE

**Thinking About the Group**
Write a prayer for one person in the group who is trying to share his or her faith more openly:

**Thinking About Yourself**
Are you proclaiming the Gospel through your words and life-style? Are you "fanning into flame" your spiritual gifts? Give examples of how you are, or will be, following these commands:

**Thinking About Your World**
Pray for one person in your sphere of influence who has not yet come to the knowledge of Christ. Write this prayer here:

# DEAR SMALL GROUP LEADER:

*Picture Yourself As A Leader.*

List some words that describe what would excite you or scare you as a leader of your small group.

## A Leader Is Not...
- ☐ a person with all the answers.
- ☐ responsible for everyone having a good time.
- ☐ someone who does all the talking.
- ☐ likely to do everything perfectly.

## A Leader Is...
- ☐ someone who encourages and enables group members to discover insights and build relationships.
- ☐ a person who helps others meet their goals, enabling the group to fulfill its purpose.
- ☐ a protector to keep members from being attacked or taken advantage of.
- ☐ the person who structures group time and plans ahead.
- ☐ the facilitator who stimulates relationships and participation by asking questions.
- ☐ an affirmer, encourager, challenger.

❏ enthusiastic about the small group, about God's Word, an‹ about discovering and growing.

## What Is Important To Small Group Members?

❏ A leader who cares about them.
❏ Building relationships with other members.
❏ Seeing themselves grow.
❏ Belonging and having a place in the group.
❏ Feeling safe while being challenged.
❏ Having their reasons for joining a group fulfilled.

## What Do You Do . . .

**If nobody talks—**

❏ Wait—show the group members you expect them to answer.
❏ Rephrase a question—give them time to think.
❏ Divide into subgroups so all participate.

**If somebody talks too much—**

❏ Avoid eye contact with him or her.
❏ Sit beside the person next time. It will be harder for him or he‹ to talk sitting by the leader.
❏ Suggest, "Let's hear from someone else."
❏ Interrupt with, "Great! Anybody else?"

**If people don't know the Bible—**

❏ Print out the passage in the same translation and hand it out ‹ save time searching for a passage.
❏ Use the same Bible versions and give page numbers.
❏ Ask enablers to sit next to those who may need encourag‹ ment in sharing.
❏ Begin using this book to teach them how to study; affirm the‹ efforts.

**If you have a difficult individual—**

❏ Take control to protect the group, but recognize that explori‹ differences can be a learning experience.
❏ Sit next to that person.
❏ To avoid getting sidetracked or to protect another group memb‹ you may need to interrupt, saying, "Not all of us feel that way‹
❏ Pray for that person before the group meeting.

# ONE

## *Priorities*

Dedicated people. We notice dedicated people. They rise to the top of the heap while others settle for mediocrity. They are the "curve busters" in school because they study so much. They are the experts on TV who are paid large fees for their analyses of perplexing problems. We see some of them doing great things for humanity and some destroying the things we call important. But whether they build up or destroy, there is no question that they are dedicated to their causes.

During the Persian Gulf War, people focused great attention on General Norman Schwarzkopf, the commander in charge of Operation Desert Storm. The general knew what he was doing, and it was obvious he was committed to his cause. He also knew how to "deliver the goods." Many Americans admired this man of unyielding commitment to his charge. But few would deny that Saddam Hussein was equally committed to his cause. Whatever else history shall say about the Iraqi president, it will surely point to his tenacity in holding out for his desires. Such is the nature of total commitment.

We can be committed; and, indeed, most of us are committed to a cause. But are we committed to the right set of priorities? That is the crucial question for us. Have our desires fallen in line with Christ's desires? This session is designed to focus our attention on our calling to be committed disciples. We are to live with our priorities in line with Christ's will for us.

As **Group Leader** of this small group experience, *you* have a choice as to which elements will best fit your group, your style of leadership, and your purposes. After you examine the **Session Objectives,** select the activities under each heading with which to begin your community building.

---

## SESSION OBJECTIVES

√ To get acquainted by talking about the qualities of people we view as successful.

√ To listen as others share their ideals, dreams, and desires with the group.

√ To learn from the Gospel of Luke what Jesus means when He calls us to committed discipleship.

√ To examine the hindrances to a disciplined Christian life.

√ To encourage each other to change things in our lives in order to reflect "kingdom priorities."

---

## GETTING ACQUAINTED               20–25 minutes

**Reaching the Top**

Effective leaders give people time to talk about themselves, about the things that interest them, about the things that truly inspire them. In this section encourage people to look at those people who have been dedicated in their fields of endeavor. Get participants' responses to each question to help them see some of the qualities that those "successful" people possessed to get to the top. The discussion should give you a glimpse of what group members think important or desirable. After a few minutes of discussion, make a bridge to the material in the Bible.

### Pocket Principle

**1** Understanding why people come to small groups helps us enhance our effectiveness as leaders. So often many of us think that the success of a particular small group depends on the level of "dynamic" Bible study we offer. While some certainly are heavily influenced by this aspect of group life, many more are simply attracted by the relationships they find meaningful in the group. So, we must be sure to spend adequate time helping group members get to know each other. This does not mean we discard Bible study; we simply devote enough time to personal interaction so that the Bible study time can generate open, personally meaningful discussion.

### Optional—Portrait Icebreaker

Perhaps you are starting with a brand new group of people in this series of studies. Group members need to relax and start getting to know one another. You may wish to start off your session with a little fun that can also help people connect names with faces. Try this:

Distribute paper and pencils (or crayons, markers). Have each person draw a facial self-portrait within a one-minute time limit. Collect the papers and shuffle them, and then display them one at a time as group members guess who's who. After each correct guess, the person pictured must tell his or her name and reveal a hobby or special interest.

Optional follow-up discussion starter: **When I think of God looking at my portrait, I would have to say that God sees me as . . .**

## GAINING INSIGHT 30–35 minutes

### Following Jesus

Ask three people to participate in reading Luke 9:57-62 aloud. One person reads the narration, another the words of Jesus, and another the words of the inquirers. In this way you can give people a better sense of the dialogue that takes place. They'll feel more impact through hearing the dialogue.

❑ **How would you describe your basic reaction to Jesus' statements in Luke 9:57-62?** (This first question asks about group members' reactions to the story. We may be taken back by the severity of Jesus' statements. Perhaps we all should be somewhat shocked by Jesus' demands on our lives. As leaders, we have to ask ourselves whether we are willing to pay the price to follow Christ.)

Give participants a few moments to mark one of the listed responses. Then ask volunteers to share what they marked, and why.

Summarize the following passages:

❑ Luke 9:58—Jesus has no place to call home.
❑ Luke 9:60—Leave ordinary affairs to mundane people, but you give your attention to being a witness for the Gospel.
❑ Luke 9:62—Be determined in your resolve to follow Christ.

These verses certainly qualify to be in a list of the "hard sayings of Jesus." Yet we cannot simply disqualify them from our serious consideration. We must attempt to come to grips with what it means to make Christ our absolute, number-one priority. If we don't, we'll likely pay the price in ineffective living and unsatisfied longings.

Point out at this time that many things hold us back. First of all, the cares of this world seem to engulf us and make us so conscious of our worries that we fail to consider how godly priorities could lift us up and give us a new perspective. Or, on the other hand, we get bogged down in "doing" things, maybe even good things, but we may forget the reason for doing them. Undoubtedly, several people will be able to add valuable insight on the best ways to begin making changes toward greater commitment and wiser prioritizing.

**Optional—Mini-Cases**
You could help bring the Luke passage into the present for your group by discussing three modern-day would-be disciples of Jesus. Photocopy the mini-cases (or write them on index cards) and use them to generate discussion about what

it actually means to be a committed disciple today. Divide your group into three smaller groups and distribute one mini-case to each small group. Have participants work together to come up with a response to the questions: What would you say is this person's greatest need from God? If you were Jesus, how would you respond to this person?

❏ **Ralph walked to the front of the church and said: "From now on, it's nothing but following Jesus—no more drinking, no more flying off the handle, and no more lying!"**

❏ **Mary, a single mother, felt a sense of despair about her spiritual life as she washed the dishes. She knew she was missing something, but her four young children kept her "hopping." Here they came, asking for another snack.**

❏ **Larnell felt a call to the ministry, but he wanted to finish his engineering doctorate first, before enrolling in seminary. He knew he could always fall back on research and development if life in the church didn't pan out for him.**

After about eight minutes, reconvene and have the small groups share their responses with the whole group.

❏ **In 1 Corinthians 1:18 the Apostle Paul declares that the Gospel is "foolishness to those who are perishing, but to us who are being saved it is the power of God." In what way is the Gospel "foolishness" to our unbelieving friends, relatives, coworkers, and neighbors?** (The Gospel is foolishness to those who regard it as simply religious talk and not absolute reality. It is hard to confront such people because they simply do not see the reality of what Christ has done for them. It saddens us to see such a response, but in our relativistic world, many do reject the absolute claims of Christ. Such claims are exclusive in the sense that if people do not follow Christ when hearing and understanding the personal implications of the Gospel, they are on the road to perishing. That is hard for some to swallow, yet it is biblical truth.)

❑ **What is a Christian, according to Acts 11:25-26? Do we have the same understanding of what a Christian is in our day?** (Notice that the believers in Acts 11:25-26 were first called disciples, and then called Christians. Today, we may think of disciples as being more mature, or maybe even more fanatical, Christians. In the first century, one was either a disciple or not a Christian at all. That doesn't mean people were always mature in their faith. But they had no doubts that a commitment to Christ carried a high cost with it.)

❑ **What is the essence of discipleship according to Matthew 10:39?** (The essence of discipleship is to lose our lives for Christ's sake and be satisfied with the joy and hope that comes from that choice. The minute we strive for our own happiness apart from Christ is the minute we lose our grip on the essential nature of our calling.)

If you have time, read aloud Matthew 16:24. This verse speaks about denial of self. Explore with your group how denial of self does take place in our everyday lives. For instance, many of us "deny ourselves" when we go to work in the morning. We would rather stay in bed, but we go to work anyway. In the Christian life we may need to become more attuned to the needs of others. Meeting other's needs, then, usually means we put off satisfying our own desires.

## Pocket Principle

**2** Always promote the positive aspects of group life so people can see the "pay off" of their commitment. For example, point out the benefits of group life in your responses to the questions. Certainly following Christ involves sacrifice, but it is sacrifice done in community. The disciples were known as "The Twelve." They were a small group. They followed Jesus *together*—as we need to do.

### Optional—Quote Reactions
If some of your group members would like to go a little deeper into a discussion of the meaning of submission to

God's will, consider getting their reactions to this quote by the late writer and Christian apologist, C.S. Lewis:

> Some of the saints recommend a "total renunciation" at the very threshold of our discipleship; but I think this can mean only a total readiness for every particular renunciation that may be demanded, for it would not be possible to live from moment to moment willing nothing but submission to God as such. What would be the *material* for the submission? It would seem self-contradictory to say "What I will is to subject what I will to God's will," for the second *what* has no content (*The Problem of Pain*, New York: Macmillan, p. 113).

Discuss:
- ❏ **What is Lewis trying to say here? How do you react?**

- ❏ **Do you agree that we can only submit to God's will at each particular point of decision rather than submitting "in general"?**

- ❏ **How could this view of submission to God help a Christian better handle his or her ordering of daily priorities?**

## GROWING BY DOING                    15–20 minutes

### Considering Total Commitment

In this section, you'll help participants apply the issue of making Christ a priority in their lives. So, as you lead the discussion on what a committed Christian life would "look like," make sure people are being practical and specific. For example, people may say, "I should be more Christlike at work." But that is far too vague and does not allow them to make a specific, relevant application. It is better to encourage them to say how, or in what specific ways, it is hard to follow the Lord at work—and then attack the problem. The more specific, the better the application.

- ❏ **How would the church be different, if people took these teachings more seriously?** (The church would be transformed if such sold-out commitment were evident in most of its members. We would not be able to contain the people who would be drawn to our churches. People would be freely giving, openly sharing their commitment to Jesus in creative, attractive ways.)

☐ **What would the attitude of our families be if we began living more in line with Christ's priorities?** (Families would be transformed because their goal would be to please Christ. Husbands and wives would live in mutual submission, according to the principles in Ephesians 5. Parents would not frustrate their children. Children would be far more willing to obey because they would feel nurtured rather than driven. Bosses would be thrilled at the work ethic of their believing employees. Nonetheless, we may fear such commitment. We think we will lose something by such total commitment. We will. But we gain so much more.)

Break the large group down into pairs, or groups of three or four, for more individual sharing. Ask group members to talk about what they need to do personally in their home, church, work, neighborhood, leisure, or in other relationships to put their ideas into practice. Urge people to choose one area and be specific about how they could actually change their orientation toward proper priority living. Have them share their ideas with the group, asking for insight and prayer to make it happen.

**Optional—Sentence Prayers**
During a prayer time, ask people to share sentence prayers to verbalize their needs and desires to God. You may want to begin the prayer time by beginning the sentence, "Lord we wish to be more in tune with Your priorities in. . . ." Ask people to fill in the end of the sentence with specific applications.

## Pocket Principle

**3** Never, never pray around the circle. This is far too intimidating for those who have never prayed aloud before. Instead, emphasize that people should not feel

**forced to pray. They should sense wheth-
er God wants them to pray at this time
and not be compelled by peer pressure
or any other factor. It is their decision.**

## GOING THE SECOND MILE      5–10 minutes

This section offers group members the opportunity to think
of creative ways they could apply the issues they have studied. You will notice that there are three parts to this section.
The first part urges people to consider interviewing someone
else in their group. This can be done at home later in the
week, as a way to establish a stronger "link" with another
group member. The success of the group, in large part, depends on how group members interact with one another.

The second part of the section asks people to look at themselves and write a plan for change. We hope that people will
consider what they have learned later on to reinforce the
changes they wish to make.

The third section is intended to be "mind expanding," helping group members look beyond the group to others in their
sphere of influence. In this way group members can have an
impact on their communities.

## GROWING AS A LEADER

One of your goals as a group leader is to help your group
members develop a sense of personal "ownership" of the
group. Group members must begin to feel, more and more,
that the group really is *their* group. They should sense that,
in a very real way, if they do not personally contribute to the
group's success it could flounder. They also need to feel that
they can set an agenda that is most comfortable for them—
especially in terms of meeting place, time allotment, frequen-
cy of meeting, and the kinds of personal accountability
required.

The best way for you to encourage group ownership is by
having a "low-key," rather non-directive, leadership style.

See yourself more as a facilitator than a teacher. Do everything you can to encourage the meaningful participation of each member. In numerous small ways, let your friends in the group know that you, too, are growing from this fellowship along with them. As they sense that you have decided not to take full responsibility for the group's health, they will gladly pick up the slack.

# TWO

## *Focus*

Have you ever been told to "keep an eye on things while we are gone"? Perhaps you've been left behind while others went on a trip. The normal response to that injunction is something like, "Don't worry about a thing; I'll take care of everything."

The Lord Jesus has ascended into heaven and has, in one sense, left us to take care of things on earth. Are we ready for such a task? Or do the cares of everyday living keep prying our eyes off the Master's business? Or maybe our circumstances have brought us into a valley of discouragement, where we feel God has forgotten about our plight.

In this session help your group members learn how to keep their focus on Jesus. Also, help them to see that God has a focusing—or correcting—ministry of discipline in their lives. As the leader for this session, ask God to rivet your own attention on the Master too. As you model the Christian life your group members will follow.

As **Group Leader** of this small group experience, *you* have a choice as to which elements will best fit your group, your style of leadership, and your purposes. After you examine the **Session Objectives,** select the activities under each heading with which to begin your community building.

---

### SESSION OBJECTIVES

√ To get acquainted by sharing about interests and hobbies.

√ To learn about what hinders Christians from being focused on the Lord Jesus.

√ To understand that God's correcting discipline is a normal part of the Christian life.

√ To examine the example of Jesus as a motivation for further discipleship and service.

√ To consider how to support each other in times of hardship and pain.

√ To begin to think of a group project that will help knit the group together and accomplish something for another who needs "healing."

---

## GETTING ACQUAINTED                    20–25 minutes

### Just for Fun

Start with a focus on people's hobbies. In this way group members will be able to identify common interests and, consequently, further discussion will be generated during the informal times of the meeting. So, while this beginning may not seem to be intimately connected with the Bible study portion of the meeting, it does serve an important purpose. In actual fact, however, this opening does introduce the Bible study. The topic is "getting the right focus" upon Jesus Christ, according to Hebrew 12:1-13. So, in our focus on hobbies we are thinking about what it takes to attract and hold our attention.

### Pocket Principle

**1** When you find that it will take too much time to allow everyone to share a personal response to a question, multiply your efforts by dividing into smaller buzz groups. Then have someone from each small group report to the large group to help everyone get a feel for what others discussed.

Notice that the questions inquire about *accomplishments* related to interests and hobbies. This approach gives the opportunity to rejoice in the accomplishments of others. It would be worthwhile to ask people to bring evidence of their accomplishments in their hobbies by, for instance, showing the group a woodworking piece or pictures of a garden, etc. People feel affirmed when we recognize their accomplishments, rejoicing in what they rejoice in.

Note that the transition question asks us to think about why it is difficult to fix our eyes on Jesus. This is a sort of "teaser" question. It gets us into the topic of the Bible study.

**Optional—Order Survey**
Get your adults thinking about the difference between having our lives "in order," or "together," versus constantly searching for direction or losing track of goals and priorities. Say: **Think about your desk at work, or your bedroom closet at home. How would you describe it?** Read the following list of possible responses aloud for participants to indicate their responses with raised hands:

❏ Piled high: Look out!
❏ Neat, clean: Look at the sheen.
❏ Time to start over: Bring on the dynamite!
❏ Needs a little straightening.
❏ Other:

Have volunteers explain their responses, and then discuss:

❏ **How could the state of a person's desk or closet indicate something about that person's state of inner "order," or ability to focus and concentrate?**
❏ **When you think of your sense of mission in your spiritual life, would you say it is "focused" or "scattered"? Explain.**

GAINING INSIGHT                    30–35 minutes

**Focusing on Jesus**
Ask people to volunteer to read aloud Hebrews 12:1-13. You

**95**

may want to have three different people read one paragraph each.

## Pocket Principle

**2** In the same way you avoid "praying around the circle," it's also best not to call upon a person unless you (1) know he/she can do what you have asked, and (2) know he/she doesn't mind being called on at this time. While it may not seem unreasonable to "call on people" to read a text of Scripture, it is not wise unless you know they can do it and don't mind doing it. Not everyone can read well, and you don't want to embarrass anyone in the group. So, ask for volunteers.

In the "Behaviors/Attitudes" chart exercise, notice that there are two types of restrictions that inhibit race running. The first are simply hindrances that are not inherently sinful. While you may be able to come up with your own list, here are some suggestions: sports, TV, excessive busyness, "cocooning," etc. In short, these behaviors and attitudes could be anything that keeps us from focusing on the Lord Jesus. On the other hand, the author of Hebrews suggests that sin also "entangles" us. It is not hard to see that when we fall into sin we are no longer helpful to the cause of Christ. Unfortunately, that is all too clear in the light of public scandals with TV evangelists. Their private lives have left much to be desired and have caused their Christian witness to be derided in the public eye.

### Optional — Questions for Discussion
After your group members have had a chance to fill in their charts, you may wish to discuss one or more of these questions:

❏ How can a normally "good" thing become "sinful" to a person striving for a clearer focus on Christ? Give a personal example.

❑ How do you view your need to give significant time to family and work concerns? How do these things fit into your goal of running a successful Christian race?

❑ What is your view of recreation and leisure? Is God a part of these areas of your life? Explain.

❑ As you view the list of items on your chart, what issue emerges as being the major obstacle to your continued growth in Christ? What are your thoughts about how to overcome that obstacle through God's grace?

❑ In Hebrews 12:2 we have our goal marked out for us. What is that goal? (The goal set before us is to finish our own race. This may involve a specific mission, as was the case with Jesus' saving work on our behalf. Or the goal may be primarily to maintain the quality of the general "race," or witness, in our lives. In both cases, we are to run to win. We are to aim for faithful living without hindrances or entanglements.)

❑ How are Christ's character and actions described in Hebrews 12:2-3? (Jesus' example is to provide encouragement for us. Two areas are worth highlighting from this text, His character and His actions. With regard to His character, Jesus is the author and perfecter of our faith. Our faith rests upon His faithfulness, which He demonstrated by going to the cross in obedience to God the Father. He endured terrible treatment, kept His eye on the will of God and the reward that was waiting for Him: the joy of doing God's will. It was hard. And because Jesus was fully human, His example holds great meaning for us.)

❑ What word is repeated so often in Hebrews 12:5-11? (The repeated word is "discipline." Point out that hardship is one way God provides discipline. God has not abandoned us but, rather, He is assuring us that we are His children. God knows best. He is the perfect father.)

## Pocket Principle

**3** As you discuss group members' diary entries, remember that analogies are helpful, but sometimes they can obscure the meaning of a biblical truth for people in certain situations. For example, the concept that God is a father is wonderfully vivid and soothing for those who have had good earthly fathers. This may not be so helpful for others with abusive fathers. So you may want to ask someone who has had a great experience with an earthly father to describe how that has enhanced his or her life. But be cautious here, knowing that others may have difficulty with the concept. This does not mean the concept is not valid, only that some people must look past the poor performance of their earthly fathers to see what God means by being called Father. The definition of what a good father is will be seen by how God treats us, not by dwelling on the imperfect human example.

☐ **Based on Hebrews 12:9-10, what are the results and qualities of human discipline and God's discipline?** (Human discipline should lead to respect for our parents and is done as parents think best. God's discipline leads to eternal life for us and is always done for our good. Stress that the ultimate result of God's discipline is a sharing in His holiness. It leads to a "harvest of righteousness and peace" for us. Our problem is that though our inner selves really want this, our outward "egos" often *don't* really want this [see Romans 7]! But as we offer ourselves to God's holiness we will find that our own lives are strengthened and we will serve as healing agents for others.)

## GROWING BY DOING          15–20 minutes

### "Hard" Things

Getting personal may be difficult for some groups but is vital for the overall health of the people. Try to find out what is going on in people's lives. Perhaps some are experiencing severe hardship, others only mild difficulties. Your goal is to develop a group in which people help each other. Thus, the first question in this section focuses on writing down a few of the hard things that are going on. The second question asks people to open up with one another. The group is to break down into groups of two or three in order to share more personally and intimately.

A result of this section should be that there will be concerted prayer for others. If your group is used to praying aloud, ask that people pray for one another in their small groups. Be sensitive here, however, to those who are not used to praying aloud. You may want to ask a "secretary" from each group to compile a list of requests to be prayed for by the leader at the close of the session. Or, you may wish to have a volunteer from each group pray.

The other result you wish to see from this activity is to have people linking up to help each other. This may happen as people share. Group members can ask each other: "Is there something I can do to alleviate your hardship?" Sometimes the answer will be "yes," sometimes it will be "no." Nevertheless, the offers of support will be mutually encouraging.

## GOING THE SECOND MILE          5–10 minutes

Encourage a further response from people in three areas: the group as a whole, the individual, the world outside of the group.

Your group might like to consider a group project. Group projects can be very valuable, not only to put "feet" to our faith, but also to bond and knit the group together. Even if nothing concrete comes from this suggestion at this meeting, you will have opportunity to put more "flesh" on suggested ideas later on (in Session 6).

## Pocket Principle

**4** Have you heard of the "pebble in the pool" method? It's a way to gently have your own ideas seriously considered and accepted. When one tosses a pebble in a pond, ripples go out in concentric circles until they reach the sides of the pond. It takes time for the effect of the dropped pebble to reach the sides. Our ideas, likewise, take time to be considered by those in the group. This will be evident as you introduce the concept of a group project. Initially, the idea may not be received with enthusiasm. But later on, you probably will get a better hearing.

The **Thinking About Yourself** section is very personal. It deals with the inner recesses of a person's life. Urge people to look at it and deal with it before the Lord, perhaps in a moment of silence. Don't expect people to share their responses, unless certain volunteers feel comfortable doing so.

The **Thinking About Your World** section asks group members how they could encourage someone outside the group who is undergoing trials. The message of Hebrews 12:1-13 could be of immense benefit to someone they know.

## GROWING AS A LEADER

Examine the structure of the group meeting time. Ask the following questions:

❑ Did I start on time?

❑ Did I allow sufficient time for **Getting Acquainted?**

❑ Have I been sensitive to needs/concerns of group members?

❑ Have I moved people along even if we didn't get finished with every question?

**100**

❏ Did I make sure we addressed the application section, **Growing By Doing?**

❏ Did I break up the group to facilitate sharing?

❏ Did I end on time?

These questions will lead you to be aware of the importance of structuring the meeting to both facilitate sharing and to attend to important aspects of small group life.

# THREE

## *Lifestyle*

Along the Italian Riviera it's considered quite essential to have an outside balcony. The balcony is apparently so important that people in homes unable to afford this structure often display a *painted* substitute. To make these "fake balconies" appear more realistic, some even include the family wash! A visitor walking close to one of these houses eventually becomes aware of a significant discrepancy between appearance and reality.

In many Christian's lives there is a similar kind of discrepancy, a difference between reality and life-style: the reality of our life "hid in Christ" and our daily struggle to "paint on" holiness by our own willpower. If only we could see the reality of who Christ is and feel the full impact of what He has done for us! Then our behavior would change. We could bring it in line with God's desires.

As **Group Leader** of this small group experience, *you* have a choice as to which elements will best fit your group, your style of leadership, and your purposes. After you examine the **Session Objectives,** select the activities under each heading with which to begin your community building.

## SESSION OBJECTIVES

√ To get acquainted by talking about what a "typical" day looks like.

√ To discuss the standards that God has for our behavior.

√ To realize our true identity in Christ and see how this affects our outlook on life.

√ To look at our lives to see how much they are in tune with God's desires.

√ To examine our goals and interests to decide whether they need adjusting.

√ To encourage one another to follow through on appropriate changes in our lives.

## GETTING ACQUAINTED     20–25 minutes

### The Typical Day

Note that the questions in the Getting Acquainted section deal with each person's typical day. The focus is on what a person did at 10 A.M. that day.

### Pocket Principle

**1** In general, group discussion questions should carefully avoid the issue of career. While knowing what career people have probably will come out in time, not all will have a definable "career." Value judgments about people should not be made based on the way we tend to place higher values on certain careers than others. The focus should remain on people as people, not on what career they have chosen. The most important thing about people is not what they "do for a living," but *who they are,* and *what they are becoming.*

This section has a transition question. People should begin to see how their choice of lifestyles already has some redeeming qualities. We should not always think that we are deficient in every way in our lives. God has already brought about some wonderful growth in our lives. So, we can joyfully acknowledge this as God's goodness and grace.

**Optional — Agree/Disagree/Discuss**
Tell group members that you are going to read a series of "controversial" statements about Christian lifestyle. After reading each one, ask for a show of hands indicating whether people agree or disagree with the statement. Use the questions as the basis for a discussion on Christian lifestyle by asking for extended explanations of people's responses after all questions have been asked.

1. "Christians should at least act like they are 'victorious' over trials or sin whether they feel like it or not."

2. "A truly committed Christian will be known for a lifestyle that seems somewhat peculiar."

3. "True disciples of Jesus never fit into the crowd."

4. "A committed Christian will often overlook the questionable habits of a neighbor in order to build a closer relationship with that person."

5. "A Christian lifestyle avoids the emotional side of life while concentrating on the facts of the Gospel message."

## GAINING INSIGHT                    30–35 minutes

**A Heavenly Mind-set**
The first four verses of Colossians 3 contain some lofty truths. The questions at the beginning of the Gaining Insight section will help elucidate and clarify some of these truths. They are very important to our goal of more effectively "setting our minds on things above."

Christ is seated at the Father's right hand. This is the seat of glory, power, and authority. It is further evidence that God is desiring to establish His kingdom fully in the universe. However, many of us do not view our lives from this heavenly, kingdom perspective. We can try, however, to take steps in this direction. Thus, when it is asked how our attitudes toward relationship, frustrations, and the sickness or death of a loved one would change, it is important to stress that our attitudes can be transformed by a new mind-set.

❑ **Notice that the Apostle Paul says "you died" (v. 3); therefore, "put to death" (v. 5) certain things. In what way are you "dead" and in what way are you apparently not dead?** (Paul considers us to be "dead" in the sense that when Christ died, we were there by substitution. So, we do not have to respond to worldly pleasures as we once did, since now we are, from a heavenly point of view, dead. Therefore, we can put to death those things that hinder a holy lifestyle. Sin no longer holds sway as it did when we were outside of a relationship with Christ. The bondage has been broken. However, we still feel very much alive to temptation. Our flesh has not yet felt the full freedom of the kingdom life. We now can make a choice to not follow the flesh but to follow Christ in those very practical ways suggested in Colossians 3:5-11.)

❑ **In Colossians 3:5-9 we find a list of certain behaviors that Paul urges us to put to death. What would most people in your world of influence say if you urged this "inner assassination project" on them?** (Society would not be very happy if we urged everyone to follow these commands. That is not to say that it wouldn't be helpful. It would be helpful if people followed God's standards. But they have not found the freedom from sin that comes through saving identification with Christ.)

❑ **Why is greed equated with idolatry in this passage?** (Greed is identified with idolatry because so many seem to "bow at the feet" of possessions. This makes the accumulation of things the object of their "worship.")

❑ **In what ways do Christians lie to each other?** (Do believers lie? Paul states that, indeed, they do. Probably most would not tell a blatant lie. But we do stretch the truth. We must come to terms with our tendency to make things look better [or sometimes worse] than they really are. We also have a tendency in Christian gatherings, even in small groups, to put on a mask of "everything is alright" when, down deep, things are not. This is a subtle way of lying.)

**Optional — Brainstorming for Greater Transparency**
Perhaps your group feels ready to tackle, more directly than usual, this problem of subtly holding back the truth about their lives. Let your group members know that no one is expected to "lay everything out on the table" in a crass or manipulative way (that can happen, too!). However, inquire whether any in the group sense that they would like to work at knowing each other more deeply, on a more intensely personal level. Discuss with one another how to best make a start in that direction.

You could try a brainstorming session, asking for "solutions" to this problem: **We'd like to be more honest with one another when we meet, but we're a bit afraid. How can we move to a deeper level of sharing about our lives as we really live them?**

Participants could respond verbally. Or they could jot down responses on index cards and place them in a pile. A volunteer could take them home and type the anonymous responses on a sheet of paper to be photocopied, distributed, and discussed at the next meeting.

## Pocket Principle

**2** The best way of teaching what it means to follow a command of the Lord is to model obedience yourself. Group members will sense that you have a heart ready to change and that your actions are ready to be changed, too. In this way, you provide an example to others in your attitudes and actions. Even your overall demeanor can be a teaching point for others. If you are worried about something, for example, don't pretend that everything is fine. Share your own

**personal concerns and spiritual struggles with the group and ask for prayer.**

## GROWING BY DOING          15–20 minutes

The "Heavenly Factor" survey exercise is quite personal. Your group may be able to share their responses openly, other groups may not. This kind of reflection is very important, even though it is uncomfortable. Perhaps it will be best to focus group discussion on the questions to be answered in groups of three or four people each: how people can think more appropriately and change their lifestyles to keep them more in tune with Colossians 3:1-11. Ask people to be immensely practical in their plans. Then gather everyone in the large group and have several people offer prayers of commitment out aloud.

## GOING THE SECOND MILE          5–10 minutes

**Thinking About the Group**

Encouragement is the theme of this section. We want others to be spurred on to living lives of devotion to the Lord Jesus. Group members are asked to plan to do something that will help lead others to make the right choices in their lives, choices that reflect kingdom attitudes. Suggest that people dedicate themselves to regular prayer for one member of the group, or write a note of encouragement and send it to a group member. These actions will go far to knit the group together and to bring about the kingdom life in your group.

**Optional—Affirmation Exercise**

You may wish to make your closing activity an opportunity for people to affirm the witness that they already see shining through one another's lifestyles. Distribute white or gold construction paper, pencils, and safety pins. Ask group members to cut out a star and think about a quality in the life of another group member that identifies that person (or the person's family) as one whose heart is set on things above. Have participants mingle for a few minutes as they pin the stars on each other while saying: **I see heaven shining through in your life because of your _____.**

The content of the affirmation could be very simple, yet meaningful. (Note: Group members could write slogans on the stars before giving them out. For instance: "You're a star on God's team.")

## GROWING AS A LEADER

Maintaining healthy group life can be challenging! Yet avoid the temptation to feel that it's all on your shoulders. *This is God's group.* And God, through the Holy Spirit, has supplied your group with everything it needs to function as a vital, growing fellowship of believers.

However, sometimes groups do suffer because they fail to develop feelings of closeness among the members. One way to attack this potential problem from the beginning is to recognize that a study group normally consists of three main elements: textual study, mutual support giving, involvement in mission. Use the first few weeks of your group to major heavily on support and group building activities. Then, gradually build in more Bible study as the weeks go by. When the group has experienced significant success in these areas, and members feel a genuine sense of nurture and spiritual growth, they will begin to think about how to share what they have with others in creative ways. This is when a greater emphasis on mission and outreach will naturally come into play.

# FOUR

## *Relationships*

There are some people in all our lives that stretch our relational patience! That doesn't mean we don't love them. It just means that they have a tendency to call just at the "wrong" time or drop in when we least need them. If we weren't so nice, we might turn around and walk in the other direction every time we saw them coming. However, we know that God expects a bit more patience and understanding than that. God has specific plans and desires for our lives in this wonderful, though difficult, area of relating to other people.

In this session we will look at some of the so-called "One Another" commands. While we will not have time to deal with all of them, we can certainly address some of them. This is a great chance to work aggressively on relationships among your group members. Pray that God will give your group members the courage to be vulnerable and lovingly honest as they discuss their relationships with one another.

As **Group Leader** of this small group experience, *you* have a choice as to which elements will best fit your group, your style of leadership, and your purposes. After you examine the **Session Objectives,** select the activities under each heading with which to begin your community building.

---

**SESSION OBJECTIVES**

√ To encourage sharing about group members' relationships.

√ To explore the Bible's guidelines for harmonious relationships among believers.

√ To realize that they must take the initiative in bringing greater harmony to their interpersonal relationships.

√ To help people make positive changes in their patterns of relating.

√ To analyze group life and plan appropriate actions to help the group develop unity, trust, and openness.

---

## GETTING ACQUAINTED     20–25 minutes

**Pocket Principle**

**1** During the first few weeks of your study, don't assume everyone knows each other's names. In fact, it is best to assume they don't. Name tags can be very useful tools in solving this problem. Don't hesitate to use them until you are sure, by careful observation, that everyone is interacting on a comfortable, first-name basis.

**Getting Along**

Begin by asking people to tell about a positive relationship they have with someone. They can tell what makes the relationship so good. This introduces the session topic while also providing more information about individuals. We learn a lot about each other when we see what kinds of relationships we have with others. We also will find out, through this **Getting Acquainted** time, what makes for a poor relationship. Sometimes negative examples serve as useful tools for teaching.

Note that the question about the strained relationship does not ask for a name. Nor should you. Let the group members

**110**

know that they can analyze a painful or stressed relationship for its characteristics — with the rule that no names are to be shared.

The "transition question" asks people to list some principles for strengthening relationships. This is a preliminary list that we will add to, modify, or adopt later.

**Optional — Sentence Completions**
As an alternative or supplemental opening activity, photocopy the sentence completion statements below, and distribute them to group members to work on in silence. (Or: Read each statement aloud and give participants a few moments to jot a response on the inside back cover of their study guides.)

❏ The most satisfying thing about my relationships with other Christians is

❏ The one thing that really bothers me about Christian relationships is

❏ If I could put in one sentence my "solution" to conflict among Christians, the sentence would read

After your group members have responded to each question, generate discussion by asking volunteers to share their responses and expand on them with examples. Then ask: **In your opinion, is it easier or harder to get along with Christians than with non-Christians? Explain.**

## GAINING INSIGHT                    30–35 minutes

**Oriented to Others**
This lesson is a bit different from the others in that the Scripture passages are not from one book of the Bible but

from two. Also, these are isolated commands. However, the fact that we have removed them from their contexts does not change their validity as injunctions for us to follow. (If possible, do read aloud the contexts of these verses, perhaps using various Bible translations.)

The two key words found in all of these passages are *one another*. Functioning according to these commands can transform group life. Your role as leader is to help the group do just that—to help members get involved in a transforming process that will move them into stronger, more mutually encouraging relationships.

The method is simple. Ask people three questions: What is the command? How can we do this command in the group? What makes doing this command difficult in our culture? These questions will be asked regarding each command.

**Optional—Verse Search**
If you have time, you may wish to look at some of the other "one another" passages found in the New Testament. Here is a short list.

Group members could be assigned one or more passages and asked to paraphrase the key injunctions for the rest of the group. Then discuss: **In your opinion, to what extent are these commands realistic for the twentieth-century church? Which ones are the easiest to do? Which are the hardest? Why?**

❑ John 13:34—Love one another.
❑ Romans 14:13—Don't judge one another.
❑ Romans 15:7—Receive one another.
❑ 1 Corinthians 6:7—Don't go to law against one another.
❑ 1 Corinthians 12:25—Care for one another.
❑ Galatians 5:13—Serve one another.
❑ Galatians 5:26—Don't envy one another.
❑ Ephesians 4:32—Be kind and forgiving toward one another.
❑ Ephesians 5:21—Submit to one another.
❑ Colossians 3:9—Do not lie to one another.
❑ Colossians 3:13—Bear with one another.

❏ Colossians 3:16—Teach and admonish one another.
❏ 1 Thessalonians 4:18—Comfort one another.
❏ Hebrews 3:13—Exhort one another daily.
❏ James 4:11—Do not speak evil of one another.
❏ James 5:9—Do not grumble against one another.
❏ James 5:16—Confess your trespasses to one another.
❏ 1 Peter 4:9—Be hospitable to one another.
❏ 1 Peter 4:10—Minister your gifts to one another.

Romans 12:10 contains the commands to honor one another and to be devoted to one another. Doing these commands in the group might include:

❏ Showing up on time
❏ Listening to one another empathetically
❏ Being consistent in attendance
❏ Providing care, counsel, and other forms of comfort when needed
❏ Offering to help others in practical ways
❏ Adopting others' suggestions when possible

Our culture does not encourage us to do these things, however. We are more apt to think we ourselves are most important and gauge every event on how it affects us. We are trained to look out for "Number One."

Romans 15:7 speaks about accepting one another. This includes:

❏ Seeing others' backgrounds in a positive light
❏ Not overly focusing on another's idiosyncracies
❏ Hearing what is really going on inside
❏ Allowing someone to speak and not be judged or shamed if the comment doesn't measure up to popular "standards"
❏ Offering encouragement to all, not just those we "like"

Again, our culture is not very encouraging in these ways. It seems that we are trained to measure everything against one standard—ourselves. If people are different, we judge them deficient. If we really are irritated by their "strangeness" we may tell them, in many subtle ways, to measure up. But there is much latitude in God's church to act in diverse ways

**113**

and still not sin. Whether we wear earrings or not, for instance, is of no consequence in the kingdom of God, so it should be of no concern to God's disciple.

Romans 16:16 brings up the issue of greeting. Few people are ready for a kiss on the cheek upon entering a home, though in the first century this practice would have been common in the churches to which Paul wrote. Nonetheless, we can be diligent to make people feel welcome. We do this in our groups by:

❏ Having the porch light on at night to welcome people
❏ Giving a ready handshake, or hug when appropriate
❏ Looking people in the eyes as we talk to them
❏ Have meaningful conversations that recall heartfelt concerns shared in the group

In this area our culture is not terribly unhelpful. We do greet one another in our society. But what usually happens after the greeting? Small talk that remains totally on the surface can serve a purpose at first, but among Christians in close fellowship it should lead to more substantive sharing about the Christian life.

Hebrews 10:24-25 gives three commands: Let us consider how to spur one another on to love and good deeds; let us not give up meeting together; let us encourage one another. These are fertile topics for group discussion. Here are some possible ways a group could begin practicing these commands:

❏ Ask people to share what they are doing for Christ, and support them in their endeavors to live out their faith
❏ Listen and pray for people as they talk about their ministries
❏ Think about things the group can do that are classified in the "good deeds" category
❏ Continue to meet together
❏ Ask others for prayer and pray for others
❏ Write encouraging notes to one another
❏ Make encouraging phone calls

Because our culture is so interested in individual advancement, most people rarely think of what they can do for others. Yet we should be the biggest "cheerleaders" on behalf of other believers who are attempting to follow in the footsteps of their Savior (see 1 Peter 2:21).

## Pocket Principle

**2** As you ask group members to move into a deeper sharing of their lives, conflict can arise. This is not necessarily a bad thing. It often indicates that people have taken off their masks and are beginning to deal more honestly with one another.

Be prepared, then, to help your adults know how to face conflict and deal with it in a healthy way. One helpful technique you could share is the "ABC method" of direct, loving confrontation (see Eph. 4:15, 25-26). This is a form of response to a grievance that group members can use to get a problem "out on the table" while avoiding a personal attack. The response is: "When you do A (name the complaint), I feel B (name your feeling). Please C (name your need or want) in the future."

Note that this way of speaking is direct, but also includes the disarming aspect of allowing the offended person to share about his or her inner reactions, in terms of both hurt and desire. This is a means of being vulnerable; it is therefore also an invitation to the other person to respond in kind.

GROWING BY DOING          15–20 minutes

The guidelines that are to be accumulated in this part of the session can be gleaned from the previous suggestions on how to do the commands. Here are some other suggestions:

❑ We will make an effort to be on time for our meetings
❑ We will seek to set aside our own "agenda" in the face of a great need in someone else's life
❑ We will make every effort to listen attentively to one another and not interrupt each other when speaking
❑ We will take time to talk to one another in encouraging ways
❑ We will make an effort to greet each other warmly
❑ We will treat each other gently

**Optional – Questions for Discussion**
If you have time, ask group members to share their responses to the following questions:

❑ **How do you feel about the idea of our group working toward more harmonious relationships?**

❑ **How much of our success will be dependent on our own individual, spiritual growth?**

❑ **What, in your opinion, is our group's key obstacle to developing closer relationships among us?**

❑ **On a scale of 1 to 5, how would you rate the "comfort level" in this group – in terms of being able to share honestly about our practical lifestyle problems and concerns? Explain your response.**

In groups of three or four, have group members tell how they could employ two of these principles. This will, hopefully, move people beyond just thinking about these guidelines to putting them into action in their relationships.

## GOING THE SECOND MILE 5–10 minutes

While the last question that groups of three or four discussed related to the small group, the first question of **Thinking About the Group** addresses the same question to the individual. Again, remind people of their need to personalize the material so that they will *act,* and not just *think* about acting.

The second question will take these guidelines and apply

**116**

them to group members' most needy relationships. In this way, new patterns will begin to be developed in people's lives to satisfy some of the longings for harmony in these strained relationships.

The last question broadens the vision of the individual to include those he or she relates to on a wider scope. There may be someone at work or in the church who needs to be approached according to these kingdom principles.

## GROWING AS A LEADER

If your group meets throughout the year with no specified ending date (rather than meeting for a short-term study period), you will need to develop your skills as a "group health" monitor and problem solver. One of the best ways to monitor and maintain group health is by using a systems approach to group life. This approach gets the group involved in regular self-evaluation so that it can assess its needs and adjust its goals and methods as concerns arise. The group will function as a growing, flexible organism that is constantly open to adaptive change.

Here's how the process works. At regularly scheduled times during the year (or when special crisis situations arise), go through these steps:

**1. Gather and distribute group information.** Use a simple Strength/Weakness survey. Ask group members to write, anonymously, three strengths and three weaknesses they see in the group. Gather the responses, type them up during the week, and distribute them in the next meeting.

**2. Develop and prioritize a list of key concerns.** As people analyze the survey results, work with them to choose two or three of the major themes that come through as significant group problems (after spending some time in praise for group strengths!).

**3. Brainstorm solutions to key problem areas.** Open the session up to a period of brainstorming. Jot ideas on news-

**117**

print and prioritize them until the group agrees on some specific problem-solving strategies.

**4. Implement the strategies for a set period of time.** Decide on one or two things the group will do, during a "trial period," to begin attacking the weakness or problem areas.

**5. Evaluate the success of the strategies and restart the cycle.** After the trial period, evaluate what happened. Your group has now adapted in at least some small way. It is now prepared for the next cycle of information gathering as the systems process starts over.

# FIVE

## *Partnership*

Partnerships in any endeavor are wonderful—when they work. They can be nightmares when they don't. A partnership that works will be characterized by a sense of strength, harmony, and mutual respect. Those that don't work usually are marked by distrust, second-guessing and frustration. A church is to be a living, growing organism—the Body of Christ—in which partnership thrives and produces spiritual fruit. Too often, however, the local church is a place of bickering, backstabbing, and disunity.

Our study in this session will focus on this crucial area of partnership. Certainly this will be helpful for the group itself. But it should also benefit the entire church, since members of the group are probably members of a local community of believers. In any case, people should more highly value each other as a result of this session and develop a greater sense of partnership with one another.

As **Group Leader** of this small group experience, *you* have a choice as to which elements will best fit your group, your style of leadership, and your purposes. After you examine the **Session Objectives,** select the activities under each heading with which to begin your community building.

---

## SESSION OBJECTIVES

√ To share with one another special abilities and talents.

√ To learn about God's plan of having a partnership of gifts and abilities in the church.

√ To realize the importance of valuing one another.

√ To help people understand that they have gifts, talents, and abilities that God has given them for Christian edification and service.

√ To affirm those inside and outside of the group because of how God is using them.

---

## GETTING ACQUAINTED          20–25 minutes

### Doing Things Well

Begin with the questions about what people enjoy doing. Generally speaking, people like to talk about themselves. It is easy to get them to do this when they are confident about what they do. Because everyone does *something* well, everyone should have something to talk about. Some may feel that you are trying to get them to "toot their own horn." However, affirm your group members by saying that this exercise is one way of helping us to get to know one another better and to help us value the gifts God has granted each of us.

The final question asks about what we *wish* we did well. This is not to call attention to our deficiencies, but to show that we value such gifts, talents, and abilities in others.

### Optional—Graffiti Poster

If you have time for some extra advanced preparation, consider having your adults jot entries on a graffiti poster as they come into the meeting room. Obtain a large piece of poster board (or newsprint) and tape it to a wall. The poster should have a heading at the top that reads: "True partnership means . . ." On a nearby table make crayons or colored markers available. Encourage people to write, mark, draw, or doodle any words, phrases, or pictures that immediately come to mind upon thinking of "partnership." (Or you may simply use the chalkboard and a piece of chalk that can be passed to each person who participates.)

Make time later in the session to draw attention to the graffiti. Ask various people to comment on what they had in mind when they marked the poster. Then ask:

❑ **What is your most memorable experience working on a project with another person? another Christian?**

❑ **How would you compare the two experiences?**

❑ **In your opinion, what is unique about Christians working together?**

(Alternative suggestion: Save this activity for personal response at the end of the session. Those who wish to mark the poster could do so on their way out of the room after a brief closing prayer. Let the poster hang on the wall until the study group meets again.)

## GAINING INSIGHT                    30–35 minutes

**Life in the Body of Christ**

Read 1 Corinthians 12:1-27. This is a long section of Scripture. It may be best to ask people to read the relevant passages aloud as those verses are needed to answer the questions in the lesson.

❑ **What is Paul's desire regarding spiritual gifts, according to 1 Corinthians 12:1?** (Paul's desire is that we not be ignorant about spiritual gifts. Apparently the Corinthian community had some questions concerning the use of gifts. Paul considered the questions important enough to answer them with three chapters on the topic. See 1 Corinthians 12–14. First Corinthians 13—the so-called Love Chapter—is actually intended to teach the importance of always exercising love when ministering with one's gifts. With all the various interpretations regarding the meaning and use of the spiritual gifts, we may secretly desire to skip this teaching, but Paul urges us to not be ignorant.)

**121**

❑ **What message is communicated to you in 1 Corinthians 12:4-6?** (The message is that while there is diversity of gifts, service, and workings, there is one God. In the body of Christ there is unity in the midst of diversity. God is a Triune God, but He is one God. There are many gifts, but they are given by one God and they all function for one purpose—service.)

❑ **Who selects the gifts we are to have for ourselves, according to 1 Corinthians 12:11? What difference does this make as we look at how we have been gifted?** (The gifts are given by the Holy Spirit. We do not choose them for ourselves. Rather, we seek to discern the gifts we have by trying various forms of service and listening to feedback from others about our effectiveness. While we may wish we were gifted in a different way, God saw fit to give us what we have. So that makes a difference. We can see ourselves as valuable because God wanted us to have certain gifts.)

Summarize 1 Corinthians 12:7-13. There are so many gifts. But they are given by God as He determines. Each part is a part of a larger unit called the body. Each person has the same Spirit baptism and each is part of the church.

## Pocket Principle

**1** A group leader does not have to feel as if he or she must handle all possible questions that come up in group discussion. When we talk of things like gifts, Spirit baptism, speaking in tongues, and the like, some people may launch into a monologue about one of these aspects of biblical knowledge. However, we can remain firm by saying we do not want to get off track. We wish to glean some basic truths from this guided study that are beyond dispute in the minds of most Christians. Perhaps at another time we will be able to take a closer look at these more controversial issues.

**Remember: A leader leads. Sometimes this means asking people to put off questions and comments for another time.**

Summarize 1 Corinthians 12:14-20. The principle communicated here is simple—we must not devalue ourselves if we do not sense we have one of the so-called "important" gifts. We still belong to the body and must learn to value our gift as important to its healthy functioning.

Summarize 1 Corinthians 12:21-26. The principle here is the flipside to what was offered in 12:14-20. Paul urges people to not value themselves more highly than others who may not have the "important" gift that they have. There ought not be a spirit of arrogance in the church over giftedness.

The implications are obvious: We are the body of Christ. Nothing can change that. Therefore, we should act like it. We must value one another's gifts, talents, and abilities. We must show equal concern for one another. There are no "important" gifts and "unimportant" gifts. They are all, equally, vital gifts to the church.

Having a sense of unity in the midst of diversity is tricky. There are things which we can hold to without wavering. The historic creeds of the faith, for instance, are central and non-negotiable. On the other hand, certain things are not central to the Christian Gospel. Whether we use piano or guitar in worship surely is not crucial. Whether a church has pews or chairs is not vital. There are so many areas in church life where it seems that the nonessential items are disputed while the essentials are ignored.

## GROWING BY DOING          15–20 minutes

The exercises here give the group a wonderful opportunity to function as positive influences in the church. Each person can compile a list of people from their church who contribute greatly through their gifts and abilities. You as a leader can provide stationery on which the members of your group can write notes of encouragement. Then you, as the leader, can send or distribute these words of affirmation. The group will have made a great contribution to the emotional well-being of another and to the overall ministry of the church.

The group can then offer prayer for these individuals. It would be helpful if the group can look around among themselves to pray for those active in ministry within the group itself.

## GOING THE SECOND MILE     5–10 minutes

In this section encourage people to think about how other members of the group are gifted. Members should take time to verbally affirm gifts, talents, and abilities that are evident.

It is also important that people consider their own giftedness as a unique offering to the church. Urge people to think in ways that are in line with Paul's teaching surrounding 1 Corinthians 12: Neither ignoring or devaluing our gifts, nor being arrogant because of them.

Ask members of the group to consider how to develop a stronger attitude of encouragement and affirmation as they view others in their own churches.

## GROWING AS A LEADER

Second Timothy 2:2 reads—"And the things you have heard me say in the presence of many witnesses entrust to reliable men who will also be qualified to teach others." One of your goals as a group leader is to expand your ministry by discipling others into group leadership positions. Be on the lookout for those open to small group leadership training, then work yourself out of a job in your current group—in order to start another one!

Who should you target for personal discipleship in this area? The best candidates have one or more of these characteristics:

**1. They are teachable.** Those who aspire to lead and teach others must be constantly aware of their own need to receive ongoing guidance from a spiritual mentor. No leader of Christians should be absolutely without accountability in the area of personal spiritual growth. So look for people who accept your guidance and counsel with joy.

**2. They are theologically grounded, but open to others' perspectives.** There's nothing worse than a group leader with a narrow point of view, or with a theological "axe" to grind. Of course he or she must uphold foundational doctrinal truth. Nevertheless, small group leaders must be open to at least hearing whatever "weird" or "strange" opinions less biblically informed participants may offer (especially from nonbelievers in the group). Many opportunities for gentle correction and guidance will present themselves to a wise leader during the course of a study series.

**3. They are genuinely interested in people.** We tend to go after the budding biblical scholars as our prime discipleship targets. We see such people constantly studying, constantly raising intriguing issues and questions about the biblical text. But such people may be *too* bookish to lead a group effectively! Are they just as interested in understanding the critical aspects of human personality and group dynamics they'll need to lead a group?

**4. They are often introverts.** Amazingly, the best teachers and leaders are not always the gregarious, outgoing, extroverts. Of course, these are the people that immediately attract our attention. They may be great leaders. But they also face the constant danger of squeezing other personalities in the group into a corner. Introverts are usually quite sensitive to others' inner attitudes. They pay attention to and value the inner life, which is the place where spiritual life grows. This is simply to say: Don't necessarily overlook the "shy" person in your study as a potential group leader. You may be surprised how that person will blossom if given the chance.

# SIX

## *Service*

Most of us do not operate in the halls of great power. Viewed from a world-wide perspective we may feel somewhat insignificant. Perhaps we have a certain bit of influence, but not much. Heads of governments, judges, big-name entertainers, and sports figures all have, seemingly, more power than we have.

Nonetheless, we do have at least some power. If we are parents, we have power over our children when they are young. If we are supervisors at work, we have power over those who work under us. If we are in any kind of relationship, we know our tongues carry immense power. So the real question is not "Do I have power?" but "How will I *use* my power?"

In this lesson we will look at the possibilities for using that power, in an attitude of humility, in order to have impact on our spheres of influence as Jesus would have. But we will find this an unnatural road to travel. Not many of us are wired for instant service! But it is the road the Master traveled, and He calls us to journey with Him.

As **Group Leader** of this small group experience, *you* have a choice as to which elements will best fit your group, your style of leadership, and your purposes. After you examine the

**Session Objectives,** select the activities under each heading with which to begin your community building.

---

### SESSION OBJECTIVES

√ To talk about certain things participants have valued because of the service these things provided.

√ To realize the importance of developing an attitude of service and humility.

√ To explore the character and actions of Jesus as our model of servanthood.

√ To encourage one another to adopt the servant attitude of Jesus.

√ To plan and carry out a service project within the next year.

---

 ## GETTING ACQUAINTED 20–25 minutes

**Tops in Service**

The opening question in this section may seem a little bit odd at first, but it helps make a relevant point. Things *do* serve us. Most of us can think of many things that have served us well—such as the car that has faithfully gone over 200,000 miles without any major repairs. The focus in this section is not on the "things" that serve, but on *what makes the service something that is noteworthy.* In addition, we will gain insight into the qualities that our fellow group members consider valuable. We then move to discussing people who serve faithfully. We look at their examples in order to compile a list of those qualities that are beneficial to a servant. This will serve as a preliminary list before we confront the Master and His example.

How do we rank as servants? We all serve someone, just as we all have power over others. The key concept to introduce is that we are to offer ourselves as servants of one another. This is the powerful lifestyle we are to live.

**Optional—Meeting the Critic's Challenge**

If your group members like the challenge of struggling with tough issues, ask them to grapple with this imaginary critic's challenge to the idea of true servanthood. Read the statement aloud to your group members, then go through the three discussion questions together. Say:

Suppose someone were to walk up to you on the street and say: "All this stuff about Christians unselfishly serving others is just a big farce. Everybody knows that we are all basically egoists at heart. We all do things for what we will ultimately get out of it, whether we want to admit it or not. Even the guy who sacrifices his life for somebody else does it because he knows he'll be remembered as a hero. Name any action a Christian takes—it's just because he wants to feel better about *himself*—see himself as a 'nice guy,' or a 'good Christian'—and then get to his heavenly reward!"

❏ **How might you respond to this person?**

❏ **Is there some truth to the idea that we are egoists at heart? Explain.**

❏ **In your opinion, can our motives ever be completely pure?** (Note: for the basis of a good response to this critic, see C.S. Lewis' famous sermon: "The Weight of Glory." Perhaps one of your group members would like to read the sermon during the week and report on it at a future meeting.)

GAINING INSIGHT                                    30–35 minutes

**Pocket Principle**

**1** Predictability breeds boredom. If you find yourself always using one method of teaching, leading, or guiding your group, it can rapidly become the "worst" method. For instance, if you always have one person read the text under study, people will have a tendency to "tune out" and not really hear the Scriptures read. One way of reading the Scriptures aloud is to do it antiphonally, alternating men and women, for instance. Philippians 2:1-11 offers a good opportunity to do this since it was almost certainly read in this fashion as a form of worship in the early church. Give it a try!

### An Attitude Like Jesus'!

Jesus is the Model Servant in this study. He is the one we imitate. Paul says our attitude should be the Master's attitude. As you explore Philippians 2:1-11 with your group members, pray that God would open their hearts to developing a more Christlike servant attitude.

Paul expects us to answer a "yes" to the implicit question about whether we have received anything from Christ. We have certainly received much in terms of salvation. We now have peace with God. We used to be enemies of God and now we are His children. We have hope, life, immortality. These are certainly encouraging!

In addition, we should be able to sense His love, His tender care. We can recall the words of Hebrews 12:1-13, teaching that God shows us His care even when hardship comes. As we walk through life we can see God's hand guiding us. Ask people what part the tenderness and care of fellow believers plays in helping them experience God's care.

Finally, Paul asks us to sense the fellowship and empowering of the Spirit. This is empowering for service. He gives us the Spirit as a guarantee of future salvation and for a seal or "mark" that says, "This person belongs to Christ."

❑ **What are the two commands given in Philippians 2:3?** (The two commands are: Do nothing out of selfish ambition; consider others as better than yourselves.)

❑ **Summarize the dual command of Philippians 2:4.** (The dual command is: Don't look after your own interests only, but to others' interests as well.)

To help fix people's minds on the example that Jesus is for our service you may wish to read aloud Philippians 2:6-11 one more time. Then you can open up the question of which of these commands have been kept by Jesus as revealed in Philippians 2:6-11. It is not hard to see that voluntarily setting aside His heavenly position and glory as God in order to become human was hardly in Christ's best interest. Yet He considered others as more important than Himself at that point. Also, being made in human likeness must have been very limiting. This was not an act in line with selfish ambition. Likewise, Jesus was obedient to the point of accepting a painful and unjust crucifixion. There was no more ultimate humiliation for One who had every right to retain His full glory as deity. Jesus set aside His rights for the sake of human beings.

God the Father's response was to exalt God the Son. Here's an important lesson: Leave any exaltation up to God Himself.

☐ **What are the principles that a servant is to follow, according to this passage?** (The principles of a servant are: sets aside own rights; doesn't use power for self-satisfaction; acts for the welfare of others; considers self-sacrifice acceptable; does what is not always convenient.)

☐ **What do we learn of the nature of Christ from Philippians 2:6-11?** (This text gives us some important information about the nature of Christ. Jesus is God by nature. It was Jesus who voluntarily chose not to exercise His divine prerogatives. Jesus chose to become human. Service was part of His plan; this was not a mistake. Jesus allowed Himself to be put to death. Jesus has returned to His position of authority. Jesus truly is Lord of all creation.)

You could consider the Resume exercise optional. However, it could be a fun way for adults to review, in a practical way, what they have learned about Christian servanthood. Read aloud the introductory paragraphs before giving group members 8 to 10 minutes of silence to work on their résumés. Then ask for a sharing and explanation of their entries.

## Pocket Principle

**2** Learn not to be afraid of silence—even long stretches of it. Many group leaders view any significant amount of silence (after asking a question) as something negative. It doesn't have to be, and your group members will quickly pick up on the fact that you are comfortable with waiting for them to pull their thoughts together. Adults need time to think, to mull over the issues raised in group discussion, and consider how they apply.

When you are sure that an extended silence is due to confusion or reluctance to respond out of possible embarrassment, then, of course, move on to the next activity. Almost always, however, waiting out a period of silence will be "productive," resulting in the reward of a thoughtful response from your adults.

## GROWING BY DOING          15–20 minutes

This is the time to solidify plans for the group service project. First, brainstorm a bit for ideas. Note that there are a few guidelines given to help in planning. The emphasis is on true service and not on building our own egos now that we have indeed served! Make sure that people are designated to actually set up all the details. After the project is over, review what was learned to see whether people sensed God building their own servant attitude.

## GOING THE SECOND MILE     5–10 minutes

Opportunities for service are endless. Help group members think of opportunities to serve one another. No one need know about this service. It is simply something that can be done outside of the regular group meeting.

On the individual side of things, help people to think seriously of how their attitudes measure up to Christ's. Ask people to prayerfully consider these attitudes in light of the example of the Master.

Finally, give people a way of having an impact on those outside the group. This time, have people write a prayer for an elected official and then, possibly send it to that person for their encouragement. It would be interesting to see if anyone receives a reply!

## GROWING AS A LEADER

Have you checked your own spiritual pulse lately? If you are regularly involved in forms of Christian ministry, beware of letting your own spiritual tank get too low! Along with your need to keep in close personal contact with the Savior through prayer and Scripture, consider checking off on these other indicators of spiritual health.

\_\_\_\_ I'm getting enough rest and recreation to balance my workload.

\_\_\_\_ I meet regularly with a Christian friend(s) to whom I'm accountable for my spiritual growth. I can share very candidly with this person about my sins.

\_\_\_\_ I attend a form of worship each week in which I am not ministering to others, just focusing on God.

\_\_\_\_ I have enough quiet time during the week, just for myself, in order to check in on my feelings.

\_\_\_\_ I have gone on a personal growth retreat at least once during the past year.

\_\_\_\_ I maintain a number of friendships with non-Christians, enjoying their company and learning from them, as I live out my Christian lifestyle before them.

\_\_\_\_ I have made entries in a personal journal during the last month, recording my thoughts, feelings, dreams, goals, prayers, etc.

**132**

# SEVEN

## *Possessions*

Material possessions can clutter our vision of what is really important. Much of our time is spent thinking about what we have or what we are going to buy. Less time is taken to consider our relationships with one another. And only a tiny portion of time may be given to considering eternal realities. For many people, the only time they consider eternity is when someone close to them dies or when they themselves get sick. But God gives us reminders about the oncoming reality of our eternal destiny. He helps us realize, perhaps very gradually, that the unseen world is more real than the visible world.

Consequently, with our focus far too much on the abundance of things we can see, touch, and own, we may become consumed by the desire to acquire. This session looks at Jesus' statements about the relative importance of "things" and how God cares for us in the midst of our feeble attempts to create our own lasting security. His words are a good remedy for the spirit of the age we live in.

As **Group Leader** of this small group experience, *you* have a choice as to which elements will best fit your group, your style of leadership, and your purposes. After you examine the **Session Objectives,** select the activities under each heading with which to begin your community building.

**133**

---

### SESSION OBJECTIVES

√ To discuss our observations of the world of advertising.

√ To analyze Jesus' statements regarding possessions and worry.

√ To adopt Christ's attitude toward the acquisition of things.

√ To urge one another to take some steps to loosen the grip that material possessions have on our lives.

---

## GETTING ACQUAINTED                    20–25 minutes

### What Is It? I Want It!

We all watch advertising, yet not all of us are influenced equally by the same types of advertising. Encourage your group members to share with one another about the effect of methods used for advertising. Together scrutinize the pervasive influence the advertising media have on our lives.

### Pocket Principle

**1** Sometimes small group leaders think that they must always get to every question in the study guide and that each person must say something about every issue. Not so. Simply try for maximum involvement and contributions in the limited amount of time available to you. Don't be afraid to say, "It's time to move on to the next question" or "I think we'll have to skip this question for now."

### Optional—Time-Limit Listing

As a supplemental or alternative opening activity, ask the group to begin thinking about possessions that are considered status symbols. Ask: **Who can name the most "status" designer labels, or brands, in one minute?**

Group members should jot (on a piece of paper or in their

study books), as many exclusive, expensive name-brands as they can recall, such as BMW cars, Godiva chocolate, Gant shirts, Rolex watches, etc. After one minute, have volunteers call out some of their responses. Then discuss one or more of the following:

❑ **What do we mean by "status"?**
❑ **How is it possible for one's self-esteem to become closely tied to possessions? To what extent would you say this is true of you, personally?**
❑ **How would you describe the Christian's true source of status, theologically and practically?**
❑ **What's the toughest thing, for you, about centering on this form of status?**

## GAINING INSIGHT    30–35 minutes

This is a very long section of Scripture. However, it is best read as one block of material. Enlist about five volunteers to read portions of the text.

**Optional – Bible Marking**
Invite your group members to mark this passage in the margin of the Scripture printed in their study books. Distribute pencils, pens, or markers and have your adults read silently through the Bible passage again, with the following instructions for marking it. Tell people to be prepared to talk about the verses they marked, and why they marked them that way.

Bible Marking Instructions:
❑ Encouraging words or phrases: ⌂ (upward arrow)
❑ Challenging words or phrases: ! (exclamation point)
❑ Most difficult parts to understand: ? (question mark)
❑ Commands to obey (underline)
❑ Reasons for obeying (circle)
❑ Portion that makes most personal impact: DPS (place initials beside)

(Note: If possible, place the instructions on a chalkboard or overhead transparency for participants to refer to as they mark their Scripture passages. Or: photocopy and distribute these instructions to each person.

The principle you wish to get across, first of all, is contained in Luke 12:15: A person's life does not consist in the abundance of his or her possessions. Indeed, the parable aptly illustrates this principle. The attitude of the rich man was that, now that he had made his money, he could rest and indulge himself on those things that money can buy. Little did he know that he would die soon afterward. How many times have we seen people saving for retirement all their lives, only to witness those people dying soon after leaving their jobs? People who are not rich before God, according to Luke 12:21, will be like the rich fool.

❑ **What do Jesus' words about the ravens and lilies teach us?** (Jesus gives us positive examples intended to build our faith. The ravens teach us that God can provide us food to eat. The lilies give ample evidence that He can clothe us as well.)

❑ **The pagan cannot claim which truth, given in Luke 12:30?** (People who do not know God, described as pagans in Luke 12:30, cannot call God their Father and cannot claim the promise of His tender, loving care.)

❑ **What should the disciple do, according to Luke 12:31?** (The disciple should seek God's kingdom and God will take care of him or her. This is a decision to think about what matters to God, and make those things priorities for ourselves.)

Jesus asks us to prepare for ourselves "treasures in heaven," where no thief comes and where rust has no effect. In Luke 12:32-34 He gives certain instructions: Sell our possessions and give to the poor; provide purses for ourselves that don't wear out. In other words, be aware that what really matters is not the acquisition of things. Where our treasures are, there our hearts are also.

## GROWING BY DOING                15–20 minutes

Give your group members plenty of time to grapple with the suggestion: Sell some of your possessions and give to the poor! Perhaps you can all agree to plan a rummage sale in which you sell something you own and give the proceeds to the poor. The alternative plan is simply to take up a collection for the poor. But use this only if the "radical" suggestion meets with significant opposition. You won't regret your decision.

### Pocket Principle

**2** Consider the effect of "radical" statements like the one about giving to the poor. Christian educators talk about the value of "cognitive dissonance" in pushing people to higher levels of reasoning about their faith. It would be beneficial for any small group leader to learn to use cognitive dissonance—wisely—as Jesus did in this passage.

What is cognitive dissonance? It's the feeling of confusion we get when faced with a seeming paradox or radical statement that clashes with our previously held point of view. For example, a leader of a group of seekers may make the statement: "Only by being a sinner can someone be saved; good people will never make it." This may immediately throw some into a state of confusion or panic. But they will be challenged to grapple with the idea to see how they can make sense of it. With further reasoning and Scripture study, they may come to a spiritual and intellectual revelation: "I can now see that salvation is based completely on God's grace on behalf of those who admit their sinfulness. The so-called righteous already have their reward."

## GOING THE SECOND MILE        5–10 minutes

The **Growing by Doing** section provided some prayer needs for others in the group. Ask people to serve one another by jotting down these needs and praying for one another in the days ahead.

Also, ask people to evaluate themselves in the area of being tied to possessions. The questions in the **Thinking About Yourself** and **Thinking About Your World** sections are linked. An affirmative answer in one will lead to action in the other.

## GROWING AS A LEADER

A lot of groups want to move into sharing at a deeper level, but they do not know how to get to that point. Your task as leader is to help the group move through the various stages of vulnerability by structuring a wise progression in the use of discussion questions. Early on in a group's life, use questions that are more fact oriented, closely tied to the biblical text. Later, gradually incorporate more open-ended questions that ask for personal response. These questions would tap into not only the intellect, but the feelings, as well.

# EIGHT

## *Continuing in the Faith*

Who likes final exams? In school we usually dreaded them. The teachers called them opportunities to share our great knowledge with them or else they used the phrase "learning experience." But the exams did show to a certain extent what we had learned. We didn't like them, but we took them anyway. The day of Christ's return will be like a great final exam for us. If we have been diligent in our following of Jesus, we will be able to stand with confidence before our Lord.

This is the final session in our series. We will consider the truth that God is trustworthy and that we can rest in His strength, power and love. Take time to pray that this final episode in your study will have lasting impact.

As **Group Leader** of this small group experience, *you* have a choice as to which elements will best fit your group, your style of leadership, and your purposes. After you examine the **Session Objectives,** select the activities under each heading with which to begin your community building.

---

## SESSION OBJECTIVES

√ To review what has been learned by the group.
√ To discuss which sessions have influenced group members the most.
√ To challenge one another to be totally devoted to Christ.
√ To gain an attitude that values evangelistic outreach.
√ To encourage each other to rest in God's provisions.
√ To begin to think about the next step in the life of the group.

---

## GETTING ACQUAINTED                    20–25 minutes

**A Review**
At the beginning of your time together, you will want to take time to look back at what has been most significant for people during this study series. If you have a large group, break it into smaller groups to encourage sharing by everyone. Be prepared to hear of dramatic impact in small ways. Remember: changes in attitude are just as important as changes in action. Affirm the steps that have been taken. If someone has given a particularly moving story, ask him or her to share that with the group as a whole.

**Optional—Sentence Completion**
Help your adults get into some of the feelings that must have played a part in the relationship between Timothy and Paul. Ask them how they would complete these three sentences:

❏ **One time when I really felt abandoned was**

❏ **One time when I really felt cared for was**

❏ **One reason I know Jesus has not abandoned me is**

These three statements point to key issues: (1) Timothy's possible feeling of abandonment as Paul described his approaching "retirement"; (2) Timothy's probable feelings of having been nurtured and cared for by his mentor, Paul, over the years; (3) our temptation to feel, since Jesus left the earth, that we have been left alone.

Discuss these three issues in depth. Point out to your adults that though Jesus is no longer physically present with us, we do have His Spirit to comfort and guide us until Jesus returns (see John 14–16).

## GAINING INSIGHT                    30–35 minutes

**Not Ashamed**

Paul is writing to Timothy in a way that gives us a glimpse of each person. We see what makes them tick. As we look at 2 Timothy 1:3-14, keep in mind that we are close to Paul's final exam; he will probably be put to death for the sake of the Gospel very soon. But he approaches this with confidence. Timothy, on the other hand, is at the prime of his life and should be of useful service for some time to come.

**Optional—Kid Paraphrase**

Invite your group members to distill the Bible truths from this passage in a fresh way. Distribute paper and pencils and have people go back and skim the passage in silence. Then have them write a paraphrase of its key points. Here's the catch, though: Tell them they must write their paraphrases in language that the average three-year-old child could understand. They must avoid theological terms without explanation, big words, and worn-out clichés to make their points. Stress that they are to make Paul's themes crystal clear and concise.

When participants are finished writing, ask volunteers to share their work. Then discuss: **How can our "Christianese" language habits sometimes be a stumbling block to our fuller understanding of Bible truths?**

❑ **What are the personal characteristics of Timothy and Paul, as revealed in 2 Timothy 1:3-6?** (Characteristics of Paul and Timothy are not hard to find here. Paul is prayerful, compassionate, a servant, confident, and encouraging. Timothy comes from a heritage of faith; he's gifted, sincere in faith, perhaps a bit timid.)

When Paul urges Timothy to "fan into flame the gift of God," he is asking Timothy to use and cultivate that spiritual gift. He is not to put it aside. The reason for the command is that God has given us a spirit of power, love, and self-discipline. These will help us in using our gifts to the fullest.

Many people find it hard to witness. Paul likely found Timothy to have fears similar to ours in this area. Paul urges Timothy not to be ashamed to testify about Christ in 2 Timothy 1:8. That is partially the reason why God has not given us a spirit of timidity, but of power, love, and self-discipline. Each of these is necessary if we are to faithfully share the Gospel with others. We need power to get over our fears. We need love to communicate the message with a compassion that allows it to be heard. And we need self-discipline to get ready to communicate with theological depth and convincing authority.

❑ **How is the power of God evident?** (See 2 Timothy 1:9-11.) The power of God is evident in the appearing of Christ, in that He destroyed death and brought life and immortality to light.)

❑ **What does Paul rest on now that he is at the end of his life?** (v. 12) (Paul rests upon the knowledge that God is able to guard what is entrusted to Him. That means Paul's life, his ministry, and even Timothy are in good hands even when Paul dies.)

❑ **How are we to acquire sound teaching?** (Sound teaching is still available through our study of the Scriptures.)

 ## GROWING BY DOING        15–20 minutes

The exercises in this section are intended to focus in on two very important areas. The first has to do with our own opportunities to testify about Jesus with others. The second refers to the next steps that the group will take to make further strides in Bible study. Urge group members to think carefully about these things.

Several members may lack the initiative to start a conversation that would center on another person's spiritual needs and desires. In that case, be ready to point group members to (1) the sufficiency of Christ for all that we need and (2) the decision to take steps of action and not simply wait around until we feel like testifying about Christ. For those who sense a lack of love, urge them to be in prayer for love for others. Or, talk about why we don't sense any love for the lost. Perhaps we are angry with those who need to hear Christ's message. In that case, we must first deal with our anger before others can hear our message.

Other group members may not know how to get started in sharing their faith. For them we need to give specific direction. Ask them to prepare their own personal testimony about how they came to know Christ. They can share it with the group. Then they can be urged to share it with a friend. The group can be a great support for these "new" witnesses for Christ.

The group should also be given the opportunity to continue studying the Scriptures, if they decide to keep on meeting. It would be good to have some specific study materials on hand. Point out the benefits the group has already received from the current study. Finally, the group can decide on the next meeting date and time. Spend time praying for the next step.

## GOING THE SECOND MILE          5–10 minutes

The focus for this section is exclusively on our efforts at being more bold in our testimony about Christ. Ask people to not allow this teaching to be lost simply because we are at the end of our study in this book. A disciple is not ashamed of the Master.

# GROWING AS A LEADER

**Facilitating Effective Closure**

Knowing how to end a study is almost as important as knowing how to begin one. Your group members have spent significant time with each other on a level that involved fairly deep sharing and a high degree of emotional vulnerability. You cannot all just walk away from the group without a planned period of "wrapping up." Arranging for this is your responsibility as Group Leader. Plan a period of time after the final session to do at least these three things:

❑ Check satisfaction levels. Everyone who was involved in the group should have a chance to give some final words about the meaning of the group for him or her. Listen carefully.

❑ Check for unfinished business. Allow any tensions that might exist among group members to surface at this time and be expressed honestly and openly.

❑ Plan for your small group's future. Discuss the prospect of continuing to meet as a small group. Make sure everyone knows what is going to happen before you leave.